Wise Guides

Fit

Wise Guides

Fit

Anita Naik

Illustrated by
Des Taylor

h

*Hodder
Children's
Books*

a division of Hodder Headline Limited

For Joe – who has the world's best willpower when it comes to staying fit.

© Hodder Children's Books 2005
Illustration copyright © Des Taylor 2005

Published in Great Britain in 2005
by Hodder Children's Books

Editor: Hayley Leach
Design by Fiona Webb
Cover design: Hodder Children's Books

10 9 8 7 6 5 4 3 2 1

ISBN: 0340884363

Printed by Bookmarque Ltd, Croydon, Surrey

Hodder Children's Books
a division of Hodder Headline Limited
338 Euston Road
London NW1 3BH

Contents

Introduction

"Don't let anyone tell you that you can't do it. You can. It's up to you. Decide to do it and follow it through."
BILL PHILLIPS, PERSONAL TRAINER – BODY FOR LIFE

Are you unhappy with the way your body looks? Tired of being picked last for team games, or fed up feeling out of breath when you walk up the stairs? Do you feel defensive (and secretly hurt) when someone mentions your weight but miserable when you look in the mirror? If so, it might help to know that you're not alone: millions of people feel this way about their body everyday. The good news is that you're about to take the first step in getting fit by working towards a body that not only helps you feel good about yourself, but also makes you feel healthy as well.

You might be glad to hear this book is not a diet book or an exercise manual. It won't tell you to ditch all your favourite foods, close your eyes each time you walk past a fast food place or run on the spot while watching TV. Instead, this is a practical self-help guide to getting yourself into shape, learning to eat healthily and having the body you want.

Read it and you'll discover how to locate your willpower, love exercise and simply how to lose

kilograms without starving yourself. This may sound
unlikely, but getting fit is not rocket science. You
don't have to be good at sports, or sporty. You
don't have to stop eating chocolate and learn to
love celery. You don't even have to own expensive
running shoes – all you have to do is give all the
fitness tips in this book a go. Try it – I promise you,
you won't be sorry.

Anita

CHAPTER ONE

What is Fit?

"I know I'm overweight but I think people should like me for who I am, not what I look like."

SIAN, 14

Whatever your current size or fitness level, the good news is that it's entirely possible for you to get healthy, lose weight (if you need to) and even run for a bus without passing out. Better still, no matter how discouraged or depressed you feel right this second, getting fit is well within your grasp. You may have your doubts, or feel the road ahead is just too tough, but stick with this book and you'll see that it's easier than you think to get in shape, change your eating habits, and get active.

Why bother, you may ask. It's what's on the inside that counts, isn't it? Well, while personality does count, hating your body and feeling ashamed of your size affects how you feel about yourself and how you behave towards others. So, you're more likely to squash your true personality, suffer from lack of confidence and low self esteem if you're unfit and overweight. We'll find out what your ideal weight is at the end of this chapter.

But before you think that being thin equals healthy it's important to know that getting fit is not just about weighing a certain amount. Thin doesn't always equal fit, especially if all you do is eat crisps and lie on the sofa. An active lifestyle and a healthy diet equals fit!

Get fit and healthy and...

- You'll feel both mentally and physically stronger
- You'll be less horrible to yourself when you look in a mirror
- You'll be more willing to try new things
- You'll gain self respect
- You'll have heaps of self esteem
- You'll be more confident in your abilities

Another important reason to get fit is for your health. According to the British Heart Foundation 22% of boys and 28% of girls are overweight in the UK. A fact that increases the chances of a whole host of health problems in later life such as heart disease, high blood pressure, strokes and cancer. Even if long-term damage isn't on your mind, being overweight at any age can cause the following:

Health problems related to weight

- Sleep problems
- Snoring
- Breathing problems

- Low immunity
- Fatigue
- Depression
- Low energy
- Bad circulation
- A change in your period cycle if you are female
- Headaches (due to sugar and caffeine overload)

Before you switch off and stop reading it's worth knowing that this book isn't going to scare you into taking action. The aim of this guide is to help you come up with reasons why you should get fit so you can find your own personal route to fitness, and while this does mean a commitment to eating healthily and doing exercise everyday it doesn't mean:

- Not eating your favourite foods ever again
- Having to join a gym or making yourself join a sports team
- Putting yourself on a diet
- Starving yourself
- Making yourself unhappy just to lose weight

Make a list right now of all the reasons why you want/need/feel you should get fit (this is your personal list, you don't have to show it to anyone so write whatever you want on it) and take a long hard look at it. Now ask yourself what's stopping you from taking action?

What's making you unfit?

 "Chocolate and chips"

JOE, 12

 "My mum's cooking"

HAYLEY, 14

 "Big Macs"

LISA, 12

 "Not being good at sport"

TOM, 12

 "It's in the family, we're all fat in my family"

EMMA, 13

Fat – it's a horrible word. It makes most of us cringe with shame, feel bad about our bodies and basically want to do the worst thing possible – diet, diet, diet! Right now, millions of us have an unhealthy pre-occupation with food and our weight. Statistics show that 13 million people in the UK are currently on a diet, with one in five admitting to being a serial dieter who has been on more than 10 different diets in the last 10 years alone. Despite this fascination with dieting, as a nation we're still getting bigger and bigger with the National Audit Office showing that 66% of all adults are overweight or obese (very overweight) alongside over 13% of all teenagers.

So just who is to blame for all the extra weight we're piling on? Some experts say the fast food industry, with its large industrialised portions and cheap deals, are the culprits because our bodies aren't made to eat such energy dense foods. Others blame food advertising, which bombards us with 10,000 adverts a year for snacks and soft drinks, which are high in fat and sugar. Others say it's the fault of our parents not cooking nutritionally balanced foods, or schools for serving chips and pizza for lunch.

Whatever you think, the fact remains that when it comes to being overweight, personal responsibility is also a factor. If you eat too much and do too little, you're going to gain weight. Gaining weight is a bit like filling a car with petrol. If you don't burn off the fuel (the food you eat) by constantly using your car (exercise), and yet keep filling the engine (eating), all that will happen is you'll build up an excess storage of fuel (body fat) that will just lie there doing nothing.

Junk nation

"My friends and I get chips or a hot dog from the take away place near our school every day, it's cheaper than school meals."

REEMA, 13

" What do I eat for lunch at school? Well usually sausage, chips and beans or pizza with chips."

TOM, 12

The large amount of junk and processed food now available is also a factor in bulging waistlines. Four out of 10 young people say that they buy their lunch from a local shop, and 15% from a fast food restaurant. The average fast food meal, has double the calorie (the energy value derived from food) count that an under 18-year-old needs for lunch.

In America the situation is worse with one in four Americans visiting a fast food restaurant every day and 60% of the population being overweight. Scientists and nutritionists continually warn that the human body is simply not designed to eat junk food and that, at most, it should be eaten once a week.

As a direct response to this the government is hoping to bring out new rules to help tackle the problem of junk food. One idea is that adverts for junk food would not be shown on TV before 9pm. Other proposals include introducing a new traffic light labelling system to identify foods. Unhealthy foods would receive a red label, nutritious but high fat foods, such as cheese, would be given an amber label and fruit and vegetables would receive a green label.

TV watching is also a major factor in weight gain. Researchers from New Zealand have found that spending more than two hours per day glued to your television screen causes an increased risk of weight gain and obesity in later life. This is partly due to a lack of activity but also due to mindless snacking in front of the TV and exposure to a barrage of advertising for unhealthy food products that makes even the hardened soul yearn for a snack.

On top of the lack of physical exercise we're also now more likely to eat out in a fast food place, restaurant or café than have a home cooked meal that's nutritionally balanced. Thirty per cent of 13-17 year-olds say that they do not eat with their parents in the evening and 39% regularly skip breakfast in favour of grabbing a chocolate or crisp snack at break time (see chapter three for why breakfast is essential for weight loss).

If you think you eat healthily when you're out, think again. Watchdogs at the UK Food Commission have discovered that so called 'healthy' meals on menus are often the exact opposite and are not only packed with high amounts of fat, sugar and salt but they are also calorie dense. Out of 141 meals tested, the researchers found that most choices consisted of cafeteria-style food such as chips, sausages, and chicken nuggets and every single one of the meals failed to meet government health targets over fat, sugar and calories. The statistics also showed that:

- 81% of meals in restaurants exceeded the guidelines for fat
- 82% of meals were too low in iron
- 79% of meals failed to meet the minimum guideline calcium requirement.

Why exercise?

"I hate sport, I hate exercise. At school the teachers only pay attention if you're good and I never get picked for teams, so I think why should I bother?"

JENNI, 14

"I don't walk to school any more because my mum doesn't think it's safe, so the only exercise I get is one hour of PE on a Friday morning at school."

EMMA 13

"I'd rather play X-Box than go outside, it's more exciting and needs more skill than football."

TOM, 13

> **FACT:** *You have to walk for 7 hours to burn off a fast food meal of a large coke, large fries and a double layer burger.*

One reason we're all larger than we used to be is down to the fact that our lifestyles are unhealthier than they were 30 years ago. Not only do we all travel by car more often but video games and computers mean more of us choose to stay indoors than go outside and be active. Physical education lessons in schools have also been cut down in favour of more academic classes, so your chances of being forced to exercise are even less than 30 years ago. A new study also shows that in general most adults don't exercise, with two in five Britons taking no exercise at all over a one-month period. This is bad news for all our health as all adults should be doing at least 30 minutes of strenuous activity a day and all under 18-year-olds should be doing at least an hour of strenuous (that's exercise which makes your heart pump) activity a day.

All of this makes one thing clear – we all need to be taking more exercise. While you can lose weight by just eating less, it's only by getting fit and being active that you'll keep the weight off, lose inches, firm up and generally benefit your heart health! You may hate exercise but the fact is our bodies were made to exercise, which is why experts believe the growing trend towards physical inactivity is what's really behind the increase in the number of people who are seriously overweight.

Studies show we are all moving less than our parents or grandparents. An alarming fact, because if you are inactive you have a much higher risk of contracting about 20 different diseases and conditions including coronary heart disease, and diabetes (see page 101).

Of course, we're not all made to be good at sports, which is why the good news is that it's activity that counts. Exercise is made up of literally hundreds of things apart from team games including, would you believe, housework, gardening and even shopping. The following are also great ways to get active on your own or with friends (see chapter five for more ideas).

- Walking
- Dancing
- Skateboarding
- Swimming
- Cycling
- Martial arts
- Aerobics
- Basketball
- Football

- Tennis
- Badminton
- Skipping

Overall, regular exercise has been shown to be beneficial for good health. On average, people who exercise regularly are less likely to develop heart disease as exercise is good for the heart muscle and encourages good circulation to the heart. Being active also helps to burn off excess fat. Regular exercise combined with a sensible diet is helpful in maintaining a healthy body weight. Being overweight can have a detrimental effect on the body for many reasons. On average, overweight people have greater chances of developing heart disease, joint problems and psychological upsets relating to poor body image (see chapter three).

What's your ideal weight?

"I want to be 7 stone because I read that's what Jennifer Aniston is, I'd die to look like her but I've got no chance I'm nearly four stone more than she is."

FRAN, 14

In order to get fit you need to start with a goal. Contrary to popular belief your ideal weight is not to end up looking like your favourite celebrity (who probably has a private chef, personal trainer and ample air brushing done to their photos to make them look so thin) but to reach a weight that's fit and healthy for you.

At puberty we all go through weight gain as the body develops, and the need for energy (food) increases. However, there's no reason to be unfit due to puberty as long as you're reaching for the right kinds of foods (see chapter four). If you feel you've gained more weight than you're happy with, then make sure you're correct in your analysis before you attempt to lose weight.

How to tell if you need to lose weight:

1. Your parents have dropped hints
2. Your weight stops you doing things
3. You have noticeable levels of fat on your body
4. You get out of breath when walking up stairs.

If you do need to lose weight don't be obsessed by numbers, especially on weight charts that are designed primarily for adults. Measuring your weight on scales every day is not only detrimental to weight loss but also downright depressing and de-motivating. If you think you need to lose weight and are too embarrassed to ask a doctor to weigh you (the best way to go about it as he has a weight chart for your age group), here is how you can work things out for yourself.

• *Body Mass Index (BMI)*

This is the scale now used by all health professionals to assess weight in relation to your height. It's more accurate than weighing scales because it tells you how healthy your current shape is, but it is complicated to work out.

To find your BMI all you have to do is divide your weight in kilograms by your height in metres, squared.

1lb = 0.45kg
14lb = 1 stone
1ft = 30.4cm

So if you weigh 63 kilograms (10 stone) and you're 1.7 metres (5'6"), you work out your BMI like this:

Square your height: 1.70m x 1.70m = 2.89
Then divide your weight by your height squared:
63 ÷ 2.89 = 21

Your BMI is 21.

A BMI of 20 is considered underweight
A BMI of 20–24 is considered normal
A BMI of over 25 to less than 30 is considered overweight
A BMI of over 30 is considered obese

• *Weighing Scales*

This is simpler than your BMI as it just involves you jumping on a measuring scale. However, measuring your weight like this only reflects how your weight changes for you. This means that unless you measure your reading against an official standard chart, you cannot assess your weight, health risk and level of body fat. Weight loss seen on scales sometimes reflects fluid loss, rather than actual fat loss, which is deceiving, and it fluctuates at different points of the month (especially for women).

• *Waist Circumference*
This test has the advantage of assessing the level (but not amount) of excess abdominal/central weight you have. It's this weight, which carries the greatest risk for health problems such as diabetes, heart disease and high blood pressure. Abdominal weight is a good way to measure how well you're doing once you start trying to get fit because if your clothes feel loose, you're losing weight.

For adult men, a waist measurement of 94–102cm means you should lose weight, while 102cm or more means your health is in danger. For women 81–89cm means you should lose weight and 89cm or more means your health is in danger. To measure your waist, make sure the tape measure goes around the belly button area.

Why diets don't work

"My mum's on the Atkins diet and she's lost loads of weight. She's going to let me do it because she says it's the only way to lose weight."

KAREN, 14

By this stage of the book you may be tempted to throw away all the food in your cupboards and go on a diet to end all diets. Never have so many of us wanted to be quite so thin, so fast. Which is why we're currently spending in excess of £2 billion a year on diet products. In the US this figure is a massive £50 billion, a fifth of which is spent on products which are totally useless and won't help you lose anything but your patience. Still, the desire to rid ourselves of weight means that many people would consider any diet product sold as the next sure way to lose weight. Ground-up shellfish anyone? The meat and fat only diet? A staple gun to your stomach? Or maybe you'd like to pray yourself thin?

It sounds ridiculous but in the last five years alone, over two million of us tried the shellfish option, a further 20 million bought into the meat only diet, 150,000 have had stomach stapling, and *Pray More, Eat Less* can now be found in 30,000 locations world-wide!

Some of these diets may work in the short term. But if you like to live a normal life where food isn't on your mind 24-hours-a-day, the only thing that's going to help you lose weight permanently is to adopt a healthier way of living, which incorporates good food and exercise. This approach has the following benefits:

- It will teach you to eat healthily for life
- It will guarantee a weight loss that's permanent
- It will keep you fit and happy for life
- It will keep your heart healthy and weight-related diseases at bay
- It won't be difficult to do as you'll be eating normal everyday food
- You won't have to deny yourself anything as long as you do everything in moderation
- It's cheaper than processed food and dieting
- You won't feel bad as you do it

What now?

Hopefully this chapter has helped you to discover why you might be unfit or overweight. The rest of the book isn't crammed full of statistics and facts about why we're all getting fatter but it is simply about how you can start to turn things around, lose weight and get fit. It all starts with finding your motivation, which if you've read a whole chapter of this book already is pretty good. All you have to do now is read on and find your way to becoming healthy, happy and fit.

CHAPTER TWO

Fit Minds

Denial

"My mum says it's only puppy fat."

LISA, 14

"I could run if I wanted to, but I can think of a million other things I'd rather be doing."

DAVID, 15

The truth is, most of us wouldn't budge off the sofa without a good kick to get us going. You may know in your heart that you need to get fit but you can't find the motivation you need to give yourself a kick-start. Don't fall into the trap of denial. You're not going to wake up one day and suddenly find you're fit and healthy and no one is going to invent a miracle pill that will solve all your weight problems overnight. Studies show that unfit children turn into unfit adults, so the food and exercise choices you make now will determine what choices you make when you're older. So, if you want to get fit you need to shake yourself out of a state of denial.

GET THIN QUICK

For instance, if you tell yourself that you don't eat much, but you're overweight, unfit and find it hard to get into your clothes, something isn't right. The chances are you may not be eating large quantities of food, but the food you do eat is calorie dense, this food is crammed full of fat and sugar. What's more, being on your feet all day is not the same as exercising. Activity means doing exercise that literally gets your heart pumping, not standing around or walking to the shops. Finally, while it can be difficult to take control of your food choices don't blame your mum, school lunches, your work load at school or your friends' influence. These things don't have to determine what you eat.

Denying that you need to change is usually down to fear. If you admit you have a problem then you have no choice but to do something about it, whereas pretending you don't means you can avoid the inevitable for as long as possible. While it's agonizing, embarrassing and upsetting to admit to yourself that you need to get fit, recognising that you need to do something can be liberating because it means that now you have a plan.

The excuse game

"I get depressed and think I'll go on a diet but then I think I have so far to go that I don't think I can do it."

TARA, 14

"I've tried everything: walking to school, not eating crisps or drinking coke but nothing works so what's the point?"

ROBBIE, 13

Of course, before you put your plan into action you have to rid yourself of all the old justifications you've been using to get by. You've been playing the excuse game. Many people stop before they even start because they just can't imagine that there's any way they can really lose weight. They imagine that while others can do it, it's different for them because of X, Y and Z. So ask yourself this – what's your excuse?

EXCUSE: I HATE SPORT, THAT'S WHY I AM UNFIT

The key is to be active, not sporty. There are plenty of people who are fit but hate sports, and can't catch or kick a ball. The key is to find an activity that suits you (see chapter five for ideas).

EXCUSE: I'VE TRIED LOADS OF DIETS AND I CAN'T LOSE WEIGHT

Studies show that mad, miracle diets don't work but healthy eating habits do. Follow the guidelines in chapter four and you'll see the weight start to disappear.

EXCUSE: I HAVE NO WILLPOWER

We all have willpower. If you can queue for hours to get a concert ticket, or painstakingly download music from the Internet you have willpower!

EXCUSE: I'LL START AFTER MY BIRTHDAY/THE WEEKEND/CHRISTMAS/THE HOLIDAYS

It's no good planning that tomorrow, next week or next month you'll get fit, stop eating fast food and buy a salad for lunch. If you want to commit to getting fit there's no time like the present. Everything counts, so even if you decide no more biscuits from this moment on, you've made a start.

EXCUSE: I'M NOT THE SPORTY TYPE

Anyone can be sporty, and at any time in their lives. Thankfully PE lessons are not an indication of what you can achieve if you find a sport that suits your personality. Not all of us are made for team games, or sports that require hand-to-eye co-ordination (tennis, basketball etc).

EXCUSE: THIS IS MY NATURAL SHAPE

It's not natural to be so unfit that you can't walk up stairs without feeling out of breath, or can't do up your usual jeans because they are too tight.

EXCUSE: I CAN'T LOSE WEIGHT

Countless studies show that if you eat less and do more you CAN lose weight.

EXCUSE: I'M BIG BONED

It's weight, not build, that's the important factor in being fit.

EXCUSE: IT'S MY GENES

Only 1% of the population can blame their parents for their weight, and yet 60% of adults are overweight.

EXCUSE: MY MATES WILL MAKE FUN OF ME IF I EAT HEALTHILY

They might at first but the leaner you get, the more they'll want to know your secrets about how you got a fit body.

EXCUSE: I HAVE NO TIME TO GET FIT

Get up earlier, or forgo your lunch-hour, or spend one hour a day less watching TV and you'll suddenly have time to exercise.

EXCUSE: I HAVE NO ONE TO EXERCISE WITH

Do it yourself, after all you manage to be unhealthy on your own. Better still, inspire some friends to do it with you, join an after school sports club (they're not as expensive as you think).

If one or all of these excuses sound familiar, it's time to stop thinking about why you can't do it and start thinking about why you can. Here's a reminder of the many benefits being fit could bring to your life:

1. More confidence when you're with other people
2. Better self esteem to feel good about your body
3. More courage to try new things that you wouldn't usually try
4. More strength to speak up for yourself in a group
5. Better energy so you actually want to do more than watch TV
6. More self worth so you feel good enough when someone asks you out

Losing weight – what's holding you back?

How to lose weight:

1. Eat a variety of healthy foods
2. Exercise every day
3. Cut down on sugar and fat based foods
4. Eat three meals and two snacks a day
5. Watch your portions

How not to lose weight:

1. Go on a crash diet
2. Starve yourself
3. Cut out a food group

4. Become obsessed with exercise
5. Eat one type of food all day

Losing weight and getting fit is, of course, easier said than done, because most of us eat for reasons other than hunger. Knowing what drives you to eat can be immensely helpful in changing your habits and turning things around. Check out the eating types below and see which one might apply to you.

The comfort eater

Comfort eaters reach for food when they are upset, sad, angry, or frustrated. Eating is a way to make themselves feel better and less miserable. But what happens is that eating often becomes a vicious circle whereby you feel bad about how you look, so you eat to feel better and end up feeling even worse because you've eaten more.

If you're a comfort eater, you need to address what's really driving you to eat. What's making you feel bad, sad or upset aside from your weight? Who could help you to tackle your feelings – your parents, a teacher, a counsellor? Talk about how you feel to friends and stop trying to cope on your own.

Then when you find yourself reaching for food try the hunger scale test. This is where you test your hunger by using a rating of one to 10 before you put anything in your mouth. This will help to remind you why you're eating. A score of one means you are not hungry, and a 10 means you're starving. If you score anything under a seven you're not hungry and you're eating for a reason that has nothing to do with food.

The always starving eater

If you're always starving when you reach for food, the chances are you're not eating enough. This may sound strange if you're always snacking and drinking fizzy drinks, but these are calories that don't fill the body up. Our bodies need nutritious food every three hours, and if you don't fuel your body during this time, you'll feel terrible and you'll need to eat something for energy (usually a chocolate bar or fizzy drink), which just starts the whole cycle all over again.

High sugar-based products like chocolate, biscuits and cake rapidly increase sugar levels in the body. When this occurs, insulin (a hormone from the pancreas) also rises and creates a cycle in the body of an energy high, followed by an energy low as the body struggles to cope. This causes fatigue, irritability and bad concentration.

To help maintain stable blood sugar levels and so not feel starving, make sure you eat small amounts at regular intervals and snack on natural foods like fruit, yoghurt, fruit smoothies, nuts and dried fruit instead of snack foods. These may sound terrible but give them a try at least once a day and notice the difference in how you feel.

The fussy eater

Do you hate vegetables, can't stand fruit, won't eat brown bread, and dislike fish? If so, you're a fussy eater – someone who won't try new food, and has convinced themselves that they can't (read 'won't') eat anything outside a group of about 10 or 15 foods.

If you're overweight the chances are it's because your diet is entirely made up of ready-made fast food and snacks that are heavy on the fat and sugar.

To change your habits be adventurous and set yourself a daily challenge to try at least one new food a day. Start small and maybe try a fruit at lunchtime, or a vegetable at dinner. If you can't face that to begin with, try to have the food you usually eat but cooked in a different form. Instead of chips, have a jacket potato, instead of fried chicken have baked chicken, instead of a burger have a chicken salad without the dressing. Experiment with food and wake up your taste buds!

The must-eat mum

If you have a mum who has banned the word diet, who won't even listen to you talk about healthy eating and who piles food on your plate, you need to talk to her about why you want to get fit.

Most mothers insist you eat because:

- They are afraid you are going to do something silly like starve yourself
- They are worried you're going to get an eating disorder

- They don't trust you to be sensible about eating less
- They think that your new eating habits will be time consuming for them

To get your mum on your side try the following:

- Tell her why you want to lose weight and how being unfit makes you feel
- Talk to her about healthy eating plans, not diets
- Ask for her help and advice so she feels included in what you're doing
- Consider seeing your GP with her for added support
- Prove to her you're not going to try and survive on only an apple a day
- Ask her to go on a fitness healthy eating plan with you.

- Talk about all the different foods you can eat and go shopping with her
- Prove to her it isn't going to be expensive or time consuming by learning to cook some of the foods you're going to be eating

Psyching yourself up

"I've got no willpower. I just can't face giving up things for good."

CAROLINE, 14

"I want to get fit but there's always something better to do than exercise."

JACK, 13

Of course, when it comes to exerting willpower in order to change what we eat and what we do, most of us score a big fat zero because, despite our good intentions, habits are hard to break. Having crisps when you come home from school, drinking fizzy colas and opting for chips with chips for lunch are all things that tend to bring us instant gratification i.e. they taste good and so make us feel good for a short while. Which is why it's so hard to opt for fruit, water and a healthy salad instead.

'Healthy food is boring' your mind might be saying, or 'I hate vegetables' or 'Why should I eat those things when I love chips?'. But, healthy food is not boring food. If you think it is then that's due to two reasons (1) your perception of it i.e. you think that it tastes and looks dull because it's not packaged as glossily as fast food. (2) You've trained your taste buds to need the taste of sugar and fat found in processed food and so healthy food tastes bland in comparison (see chapter four for more information).

You don't have to give up anything if you don't want to, and you don't have to exercise. However, you do have to take responsibility for your choices and that means accepting that if you eat badly and refuse to do anything active you are always going to be un-fit, overweight and unhealthy. If that thought fills you with dread, you can turn all of this around by simply making a decision right now to change your life. To get motivated start by:

* Not being horrible to yourself
Saying horrible things about your body and abilities not only stops you from doing something positive, but also encourages comfort eating i.e. eating because you feel sad, bad, unhappy or miserable.

* Being honest with yourself
You don't have to admit to anyone else that the reason you're spilling over your jeans is because you eat five chocolate bars, two bags of crisps and chips every day. But you do have to admit this to yourself if you want to change your habits.

* Having a realistic goal
Don't aim to look like a model, pop-star or sporting
hero – aim to look the best for your height and
build and then you won't think it's ridiculous to
even start trying.

* Telling yourself you can do it
Millions of people transform themselves every day,
and that means you can too, all you have to do is
go for it.

The ten–step change yourself plan

1. Inspire yourself

There's nothing like inspiration to get you going.
Ask yourself who inspires you and what you can
learn from them. Is it a footballer's amazing
achievements, a pop star's transformation or
someone else entirely who makes you want to
go for it and do something amazing.

If you feel uninspired, take the time to search for
a role model by reading magazine and newspaper
interviews with famous people, searching the
biography section of the library or surfing the
Internet to find out more about anyone's story you
can relate to. Your inspiration doesn't have to be a
famous person, it can even be someone you know,
or someone you have heard about. The aim is to

use their story to encourage you
to do the same thing for yourself.

If you can't find a role model,
think of other ways to
motivate yourself. Maybe
the thought of looking and
feeling good at your next
birthday-do, or being picked
for a sports team, or even
feeling you've achieved a
physical goal you never
thought you could reach
such as a 5km run. It
doesn't matter what you
use, as long as you use
something. Once you
have your inspiration
write it down, stick it on
your mirror or in your
diary and use it to get
you going every day.

GOOD MOTIVATORS

- A deadline such as your birthday or a big event
- A role model who has achieved what you're
  aiming for
- A photograph of you looking not so good –
  something to remind you why you're doing this
- A reward for when you reach your goal

BAD MOTIVATORS

- Buying clothes two sizes too small
- Telling everyone you are on a diet
- Asking your mum to tell you off every time you eat chocolate
- Weighing scales

2. Have realistic goals

Having said it pays to inspire yourself – it also pays to have realistic goals and a realistic plan. This is because, while it's tempting to throw yourself into fitness 110%, making yourself go from a couch potato to someone who runs to school and back and never eats fast food, is a recipe for disaster. Not only will you get bored quickly but you'll also be back to your old ways within the week. To combat this, be realistic about what you're aiming for. Yes, you want to get fit, but you don't have to be 100% strict to get there. Choose goals that you can easily adapt to your life so you don't have to radically change everything to get what you want.

REALISTIC GOALS

- Changing what you eat for lunch
- Walking to and from school
- Opting for different snacks
- Exercising when you get back from school

UNREALISTIC GOALS

• Running two miles a day
• Eating salad three times a day
• Cutting out all your favourite foods
• Refusing to go out in case you're tempted by
  unhealthy foods

3. Pick a short-term goal

Short-term goals are essential because if you don't
see some results for your hard work in a few weeks
then you're not going to feel motivated to go on.
To help yourself every three weeks you should aim
for a short-term goal to help keep you moving
forwards. Short-term goals can be anything from
making yourself join in a new sport, to buying a
fitness video and doing it daily or avoiding chips at
lunch time.

GOOD SHORT-TERM GOALS

• Do something active every day
• Get into an article of clothing that usually
  feels tight
• Eat breakfast every day (see page 72)
• Run across a football pitch without feeling sick

BAD SHORT TERM GOALS

• Get picked for a sports team
• Drop a dress size
• Eat nothing but salad

4. Choose a long-term goal

This is the goal that is your end result and usually stays the same. Having said that, as you get fit you may find that what you originally set out to do (i.e. get slim) becomes less important as you get near to it, or that your goal has changed completely. This doesn't matter but what does matter is that you are clear in your head about what you're aiming for. Remember, you'll never reach your destination if you don't know what you're heading for. So, write down your main goal and look at it every day.

GOOD LONG-TERM GOALS

- Get fit so you don't feel out of shape
- Get into a healthy weight range
- Feel good about your body
- Feel confident about the way you look

BAD LONG TERM GOALS

- Look like a famous person
- Reach a weight that's unrealistic for your height
- Be thin so you can be happy/get a boyfriend/ girlfriend/have no problems

5. Write your plan down

To make your goals real you need to start to make things happen and this means taking the ideas out of your head and putting them down on paper. The best way to do this is to arm yourself with a notebook and write down what you want to achieve (it doesn't matter what it is, as this is for your eyes only). Then use this get fit diary as a way to review your goals and motivations, write down tips that you find along the way, and vent your frustrations when you have a bad day.

THINGS TO WRITE IN YOUR FIT DIARY

- Your start weight
- Your goal weight
- Your starting fitness levels
- Your end fitness levels
- How you feel about getting fit
- What you're going to do to get fit this week
- Your short-term goals
- Your long-term goals

6. Take action

Okay, now's the time to take action. Write down three things you can do which require immediate action. This could be throwing away the bar of chocolate in your bag (throw it outside so you can't fish it out of the bin), or going for a long walk, or even talking to your mum about your intentions. Other suggestions for immediate action are:

- Looking up the number of your nearest swimming pool and calling them for a timetable
- Renting a work out video
- Snacking on fruit

- Ditching all the junk food in your fridge (ask the rest of your family first!)
- Taking a long but fast paced walk to the shops and back

The aim of the take action part of this plan is to show you that you can make a start on your fitness immediately. You don't need fancy trainers or health food to do it, you can simply take the first step right here, right now.

7. Make your changes a habit

For most of us the hardest part of any fitness plan is to take it from the idea stage to the doing stage. How many times have you sat in front of the TV and told yourself – I must stop eating crisps and go for a walk – only to find yourself still munching crisps on the sofa three hours later? If this sounds like you, then you need to make your new changes a habit. Habits take two weeks to form, meaning if you do something everyday from tomorrow, in no time it will feel like second nature. Try doing one or all of the following everyday for two weeks and note how it gets less and less difficult to motivate yourself:

- Get off the school bus one stop early so you can walk further
- Take a walk at lunch time
- Bring a healthy pack lunch to school (leave your money behind to avoid temptation)
- Bring healthy snacks with you to school or when you go out
- Order a diet cola or water when you're out with friends.

Remember habits grow with repetition and results. The more you do it and the more results you see, the more committed you will become.

8. Don't be an 'If only...' person.

Make your plan work with some forward thinking.
If you're going on holiday, make sure you work out
a way to do your plan when you're away (see
chapter six). If you're busy studying for exams, plan
your meals and snacks, and add three walks a day to
your timetable (it's good for your mind and body).
Finally, think about the weekend. Just because these
are your free days it doesn't mean you don't need
to follow your plan. To reach your goals you have to
make changes that cover all your days, not just
school days.

- To beat the 'I can't be bothered today' feeling,
  make a timetable so your get fit plan isn't a
  vague idea (see chapter six for more ideas on
  this).
- If you're planning to eat healthily, change what
  you do at lunchtime so you won't be lured back
  into old habits. Eat outside if it's warm enough
  or sit away from the food counter so you won't
  be tempted.
- Do your plan even when it's difficult. This is
  especially important in the early days because if
  you give yourself an excuse today, you'll find one
  for tomorrow and the day after and the day
  after that!
- Start as soon as possible. Ideas falter if you keep
  them hanging around. To become the fit person
  you want to be – start right now.

9. Work out how you're going to measure your fitness

This one's essential because if you don't measure how your body is changing you're going to give up. There are many ways to measure fitness but weighing yourself every day isn't one of them. Apart from being depressing to weigh yourself all the time, your weight isn't going to change on a daily basis, which means you're going to feel like giving up fast. Also, for many people scales are just a way to make you feel bad. So, instead of tying yourself to a certain weight, try one of the following instead:

- Try on an article of clothing that you know is too tight at the beginning of your plan, then try it on once every week on the same day to see if there's a difference.
- Find a steep hill and walk up it and see how long it takes you. Then every week walk up the same hill and see if you notice a difference in your breathing and timing.
- Pay attention to your taste buds and see if they change. Follow the food plan in chapter six and after four weeks try a type of food you once craved. Does it still taste as good? How does it make you feel afterwards?
- Measure your waist. Losing abdominal fat is good for your heart, and losing centimetres around your waist is a great indication that you're losing weight.

- Ask someone you trust to weigh you at the start of the plan but not tell you what you weigh (to avoid you becoming obsessed with your weight). Then ask them to weigh you every week on the same day and after four weeks ask for the results.

10. Stick with it when the going gets tough

We're all human and that means we all hate to do things that are uncomfortable and hard, which is why many of us struggle when the going gets tough. One way to cope is to lower our goals, give up on our goals, or tell ourselves it's all a waste of time and then run back to our old way of life. What you have to remember is that stepping outside your comfort zone (the place where you feel safe) is hard but it brings huge rewards. So tell yourself it's okay to have hard days when you slip a bit, but don't let this stop you. These hard days are temporary and if you keep pushing yourself you're guaranteed to reach your goals.

Challenge yourself to:

- Say no to chocolate for a week
- Eat five pieces of fruit and vegetables a day — even though you hate the stuff
- Run in your PE class
- Say no to chips at lunch
- Be more active and watch less TV

Of course, it's hard to do this on your own, which is why you need people to help you step out of your comfort zone. While you may not want to tell anyone what you're doing, just one person telling you to go for it will make all the difference.

Good support people are:

- An older sibling
- A parent
- Your best friend
- A PE teacher
- Your GP
- A group of friends

And remember, by supporting you their job is not to:

- Ridicule you
- Justify your excuses
- Sabotage your efforts with temptation
- Try and outdo your efforts
- Act like the food police
- Tell others what you're doing
- Bully you

But to:

- Inspire you when you feel down
- Push you past your excuses
- Turn up to help come rain or shine
- Offer helpful advice

- Remind you why you're going through this
- Join in on your off days

Finally a word of warning – be careful who you choose to tell about your plan. While getting fit is something to be applauded, there will always be people who have nothing helpful to offer. Such people will tell you that exercise is a waste of time and that healthy eating doesn't work. They will try to tempt you away from your plan and tell you that you'll never do it because they can't imagine you being fit. Rather than believing them, use their lack of enthusiasm as a motivating tool. Show them just how wrong they are!

CHAPTER THREE

Fit Image

Why bother with self-esteem?

"I hate myself when I look in the mirror. I'm fat and ugly and so I never try to look. I avoid looking at my reflection in shop windows, hide from cameras and never look at my face when I look in the mirror."

VIKKI, 14

"I'm a nerd and a wimp. I'm skinny but have a belly. The boys at school call me Mr Blobby."

JACK, 13

"I just know if I was thin I wouldn't hate myself so much."

CLAIRE, 15

We live in a world that's obsessed with how we look, so it's no wonder that most of us are anxious about how we appear to our friends, family and even strangers on the street. Everyone wants to be viewed appreciatively and yet, when it comes to looking in the mirror, it's likely you're the first to start name-calling. If that sounds familiar you have a bad body image. This is an image of your body that you dislike, or even hate, and would do anything to change. A bad body image comes hand in hand with low self-esteem. This means you probably don't think very much of yourself as a person. This is bad news because it means that if you do nothing to change the way you think you'll still have a bad body image no matter how fit you get.

You may think, so what? But studies show that the way you think of yourself and the beliefs you hold about your body affect the way you behave in the outside world. If you call yourself names or think your body shape means you're a certain type of person, then you're not only going to feel bad but also very sad inside. These two emotions may not come across to the outside world, especially if you're very good at hiding them. What will come across is a variety of differing emotions such as aggression, extreme shyness, or even anger all fired off because inside you don't feel like you're a good enough person.

You have low self esteem and a bad body image if you:

- Feel that no-one really knows the true you
- Tell yourself you're ugly and no one will ever want you
- Feel unattractive compared to the rest of your friends

- Hide away under dark
  and baggy clothes
- Act loud and aggressive
  so that everyone thinks
  you're confident
- Refuse to look at your
  reflection in shop windows
- Pretend you're okay
  when you're not
- Live in 'If only' land: if only
  I was slim/pretty/had more
  muscle/were taller etc
- Feel embarrassed when
  someone draws
  attention to you
- Tell yourself that looks
  don't matter because
  you're a nice person

Good self-esteem is essential
because it's hard to be successful
in life, in your relationships and
in making new friends if you
don't like yourself. All these things mean
taking a risk, and if you have low self-esteem
you will be too afraid to take that risk for fear
you'll get rejected and feel even worse. If you have
good self-esteem you won't be so afraid of possible
rejection because you know your self worth isn't
in someone else's hands, but in your own.

If you currently feel that you're not a worthy person because you feel frumpy, dull, boring, mean or maybe hateful, it's worth knowing that you don't have to be this person. No matter what people say, what's happened to you in the past and how others try to define you, you can be the person you want to be by simply boosting your self-esteem.

Changing your self beliefs

Step one is to challenge your self beliefs. These are the attitudes you hold about yourself such as: you're ugly, unattractive, wimpy or even disgusting. These beliefs don't just appear overnight but are cemented over time by things that we read, see and hear about ourselves. Maybe you once heard a friend comment that you had large thighs or a fat belly, or your mum said your nose was big like hers, or maybe you believe that someone of your race can't be as attractive as someone of another race. Or perhaps you idolise a pop-star and believe that as you can never look like them you can never be attractive.

"My mum always says I am pretty but I know she has to say that because she's my mum so it doesn't count."

NINA, 14

If you hold negative beliefs about yourself it's likely that whenever someone gives you a compliment you shrug it off thinking they are just being 'nice', or you get defensive. It's likely when someone says something horrible you take it to heart believing it must be true and so turn it into a belief.

It's not uncommon to do this, but to change your mindset you have to consciously think about why people say the things they do. Firstly, people do not just say nice things to be nice. They say them because they're true, or they want you to feel good, or they appreciate something. Secondly, people who say insulting things do so not because they believe in spreading the truth no matter what, they do it because they are trying to make an impact. They either want to hurt your feelings, be funny at your expense or try to make themselves feel better because they are having a bad day (remember, nasty people say even nastier things to themselves).

So when you next think something bad about yourself consciously stop and think about where that thought came from. For instance:

Who told you your nose/face/ears were funny shaped? Were they being mean or trying to make themselves feel better?
Why do you choose to believe them?
Is it even true?

Have you ever considered whether or not that thought was yours or someone else's?

To see how you rate your body grab a piece of paper and write down as quickly as possible three negative beliefs about the following:

Your face

Your personality

Your size

Your intelligence

Now do it again and this time write down three positive beliefs about each of the above.

Which list was harder to write? If it was the second list you've trained your mind to think negatively, and that's why you find the nasty stuff easier to think of than the nice stuff, which means it's time to change the way you view yourself.

What's attractive?

"Boys like blonde, straight hair and thin girls."

TINA, 13

"Girls like bigger guys – the taller the better – and with good hair."

JACK, 12

We're all affected by the things we see in magazines, on TV and through advertising. This is because most forms of media depict a certain image of beauty whether you're male or female. If you're a boy this means you're likely to be bombarded with images of men with bulging biceps and six packs, or boy bands with perfect looks, hair that behaves, and clear skin. If you're a girl it's probably long, thin models or cute and bouncy pop-stars with perfect figures. Whether you want to look like them or not, you can't help but be affected and compare yourself to them, probably in a negative way.

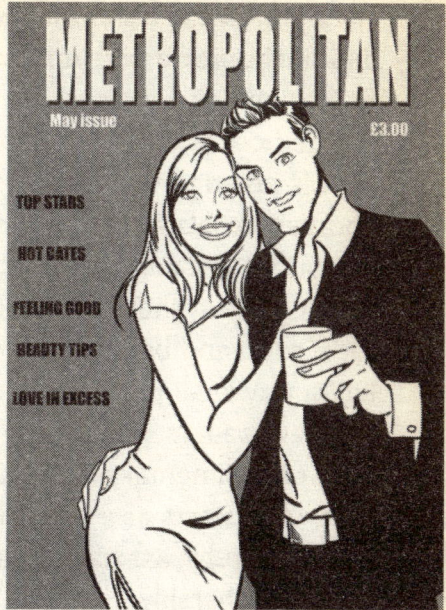

However, before you blame the media for your bad body image, remember that models are picked precisely because they don't look like the majority of us. Even so, their pictures go through some pretty harsh computer airbrushing so that they look flawless and perfect, and they never look as good in the flesh as they do in a poster. In any case, the ideal body changes from year to year, one moment it's skinny, the next it's small, the next it's curvy – try and fit the norm and you're guaranteed to be out of fashion as soon as you're in.

This is just one reason why it doesn't pay to judge yourself in relation to others. Easier said than done of course, because we all do it. We're all guilty of walking down the street and thinking that people look good and bad in their clothes or with their haircuts. We all judge people on television and in the newspapers, and usually it's in a horrible, rather than complimentary way. The problem with this is that what starts as a bit of fun soon becomes a habit whereby we start to judge everyone, including ourselves, harshly.

We may think we do it for a laugh but the reality is that it's a way to work out how attractive we are in relation to everyone else. So, if we loathe the way our body looks it's usually self-enforced.

So here's how to start changing the way you think:

1. Don't focus on the negatives

Do you hate your stomach, your arms or the way your teeth look when you smile? Are you having a fat day, a bad hair day or a geeky day? Why are you focusing on the bad stuff in the mirror? Your body is made up of a hundred other parts and your personality has even more elements to it than how you look, so do yourself a favour and start looking beyond the bits you dislike.

Self-esteem tip: Stand in front of the mirror and look at the whole picture. Keep staring until your eyes refocus on everything not just the bits you've trained yourself to look at. What stands out in a GOOD way (clue – your friends often compliment you on it)? What do you like best about yourself? Why don't you sing your own praises for a change?

2. Change the record

Listing all the things that are wrong with you is a bit like hitting yourself over and over again with a baseball bat. It not only re-enforces the point but it re-enforces the pain. Does it make you feel better to judge yourself so harshly? Of course not, so try a different tactic and make yourself say good things to yourself for a change and see how it makes you feel.

Self-esteem tip: Positive affirmations may sound like new age mumbo jumbo but consider this: if the negative ones work so well then surely the good ones work too. Say five positive things about yourself every time you check out your reflection. Say it aloud (if you're alone), in your head or write it down and remind yourself that you have more to offer than you may think.

3. Don't blame your parents

If you have an overtly critical parent who is good at crushing your confidence it can be easy to keep blaming them for how you feel. Which is why you need to be assertive and point out that they are hurting your feelings. Yes, they are your parents but this doesn't mean they can say whatever they like to you. They may not realise what they are doing or they may do the same thing to themselves so much that they haven't considered how it might affect you.

Self-esteem tip: If they keep doing it despite what you say, remember that their view doesn't have to be your view. Just as you know you're entitled to have different politics, taste in music and fashion ideas, remind yourself that you are also entitled to feel good about yourself, your looks and abilities. The next time they say something critical, tell yourself you are your own person and the person who knows you the best is yourself.

4. Be outward looking

Often people who feel bad about their bodies tend to spend too much time thinking about the way they look and appear to others. If this sounds like you, it's time to think externally. Spend less time judging yourself and others and you'll spend less time thinking about your looks.

Self-esteem tip: Don't compare yourself to others. Do this and you run the risk of either feeling smug or horrible about yourself. Practise walking into rooms and instead of immediately thinking everyone is checking you out, make yourself look at five people and think five good things about them.

5. Don't always imagine the worst

Someone laughs on the bus – do you always think they're laughing at you? If someone makes you the butt of their joke, do you imagine they hate you or that everyone thinks you're weird? Remember, unless you're a mind reader, you don't know what they are really thinking or why they are doing what they're doing so don't waste time making yourself the star of their story.

Self-esteem tip: Just as you spend the majority of your time worrying about yourself, it's worth knowing that's exactly what others do too. They are not thinking about you and your so-called flaws, but they are thinking about their own problems so you can relax.

6. Be your own cheerleader

So people don't give you compliments, say nice things or sing your praises? Maybe it's because you've rebutted them too many times in the past, or because you're always looking down and caught in a dream world. Perhaps you look too angry, too shy or too miserable so people are afraid to approach you. Being the head of your own fan club isn't a sign you're all alone, or that your ego's too large. It's a sign that you know you have worth and value. So what if someone else doesn't pat you on the back, do it to yourself! Get used to being your own cheerleader and you won't need to seek constant approval to feel good.

Self-esteem tip: People who are complimentary and positive tend to attract similar responses from others.

Improve your body language

"I never look up when I walk into a room. I can't bear people looking at me and seeing the state of my skin and how fat I am."

LAURA, 14

Now you've looked at how you talk to yourself, it's worth thinking about how you hold yourself. Body language makes more of an impact than you might think. Sit slumped over, hunch while you walk, stare at your feet and mumble when people smile at you and people will make all kinds of assumptions about the kind of person you are. What we believe and say may dictate how we behave, but it also dictates how we display ourselves to others.

The studies are clear – this is how people make up their minds about you:
55% of their view comes from your body language.
38% comes from the tone and attitude of your voice.
And only 7% comes from what you actually say.

If you want to boost your body image and self-esteem you have to start thinking about how your body language speaks for you.

People with good self esteem tend to:
• Stand up straight when walking or talking.
• Look people in the eye when they are listening.

- Smile when they say hello.
- Make small tactile (touching) gestures when speaking.
- Mirror the person they are speaking to.

The number one way to appear more confident when you're not is to improve your posture. Confident posture means pulling your stomach in, putting your shoulders back, relaxing your chest and holding your head high. If this sounds too complicated try this:

1. Stand up and imagine a string pulling you up from the centre of your head
2. At the same time imagine your belly button pulling back towards your spine (this pulls your stomach in)
3. Now imagine your shoulders dropping away from your ears and your shoulder blades sliding down your back
4. Keep your body loose not rigid
5. Bingo – you now have perfect posture!

Ideally this is how you should walk about all the time but realistically it's not easy when your natural inclination is to slump and hunch (the body's way of protecting itself when we don't feel confident). To help yourself feel more confident, try the following:

- The old model trick – walk around your room with a book placed on your head at least three times a day. This helps you to get used to holding your body in a different way.
- Give yourself quick posture reminders. If you catch yourself slumped on the sofa, sit up. If you notice you're hunched over your desk, roll your shoulders back and sit up.
- If you spend more time looking at the pavement than around you, lift your eyes up to the sky for a second and then bring them back to the centre to get used to a different eye line.
- When you're sitting down, don't cross your legs but imagine your belly button pulling into your spine. You'll get instant good posture and work on getting a flat stomach.
- Make an effort to smile at three people a day.
- Finally, walk with confidence. If you walk as if you're the most dull, boring and inadequate person on earth, that's how people will treat you.

Get immediate body confidence

Believe it or not, you can feel good about your body right this second without waiting for the moment when you're fit, thin, slim or have a six pack, all it takes is a change of attitude. The secret no one ever tells you is that real body confidence isn't about good looks – just read an interview with anyone famous to see that – but about good thoughts. The answer lies not in lying to yourself or pretending you're okay when you're not, but in finding solutions to help you look better, feel better and appear your absolute best. Here's how:

Solution One: Be positive about new ideas

This means you should have an open mind about the suggestions people give you. Instead of immediately being defensive and thinking of a hundred reasons why this book won't work for you, or why you can't exercise after school, think of reasons why you *can* do these things. If you can't think of any, ask yourself why a healthy eating plan or fitness plan *wouldn't* work for you when it works for a million other people? Be positive, what have you got to lose?

Solution Two: Have a friendship reality check

Do your friends support you or tease you about how you look? Are they your number one support or the people who put you down? To feel good about yourself you need to surround yourself with the right people. Write a list and see who's on your side. Team players are those who encourage, support and accept you. Non-players are those who tease, bully, put you down and generally are happy when you're not.

Solution Three: Don't dismiss your parents' view

Okay so they don't understand where you are coming from, they have bad taste in clothes and generally get on your nerves. However, they aren't just your parents but people with feelings and problems just like you. If you think they've never been through a bad body image phase then think again! Whatever you're feeling it's not new, people have been struggling with similar issues for years and years. Instead of assuming you're all alone, tell them what you're feeling. You may be surprised at the support they can offer you.

Solution Four: Wear clothes that do your body justice

We are all guilty of hiding under baggy t-shirts and dark clothes imagining that this hides the bulges. The truth is it doesn't and all it does it make you look worse. Help yourself by wearing and buying the clothes you want to wear rather than what you think you should wear. You have the right to look good no matter what size you are.

Solution Five: Be a good mate

It's hard when you feel bad about yourself to be nice to the people around you, so remember that horrible behaviour has the effect of making you feel twice as horrible inside. How many times have you snapped at your mum and then felt guilty, or been mean to a friend and walked away feeling nasty? If you want to boost your self esteem, it pays to start by being nicer to people around you and not taking out your anxieties on them. You don't have to be a people pleaser who is always super 'nice', just be a good friend, daughter, son or sibling when you can for the sake of your own state of mind.

Solution Six: Accept what you can and can't change

Self-acceptance isn't about thinking: 'Okay, this is what I have to put up with'. It's about changing the parts of you that can be changed (such as your fitness levels, your attitude and your abilities), accepting the things that can't be changed (such as your height, your face or your skin type) and being smart enough to work out the difference.

CHAPTER FOUR

Fit Food

Have a healthy attitude to food

Eating healthily is not just for those who need to lose weight. You can be as thin as a rake and still be unhealthy and have too much body fat because you're simply eating the wrong foods. If you want to feel good, look good, have good skin, amazing hair and generally never feel tired, you need to eat a diet that's rich in vitamins, minerals and nutrients. That's a diet that's not wholly made up of burgers, chips and pizza, but one that incorporates a bit of what you like plus lots of vegetables, fruit, protein (meat, fish, soya) and some fat. Neglect to add these things to your diet for whatever reason and you're going to feel bad.

Of course, if this is all you've ever eaten you may well not even realise you feel unhealthy or unhappy because you're so used to it. So have a look at the following checklist and see if the fuel you're putting into your body is of premium grade or cheap as chips.

Do you...

Find it hard to concentrate first thing in the morning?	**Yes/No**
Feel sleepy and lethargic after lunch?	**Yes/No**
Get irritated and annoyed by mid-afternoon?	**Yes/No**
Need to be woken up in the morning?	**Yes/No**
Only have the energy to lie on the sofa after dinner?	**Yes/No**
Reach for a chocolate bar or coke to give you energy?	**Yes/No**
Feel grumpy for no reason in the afternoons?	**Yes/No**
Hate vegetables and fruit?	**Yes/No**
Think that only overweight people have to watch what they eat?	**Yes/No**

If you've answered 'yes' to any of the above you need to get a healthy attitude to food. Which doesn't mean dividing food into 'good' (proper) food and 'bad' (junk) food. Healthy eating means eating with a healthy attitude towards food. That's eating when you're hungry not when you're bored, eating a large variety of foods and being realistic about eating the foods which are making you unfit. However, this doesn't mean denying yourself everything you like and eating all the stuff you don't. It's about achieving a healthy balance.

QUIZ: Discover your food knowledge rating

Do you think you know what healthy eating is?
To find out how food smart you really are, try this
healthy eating quiz.

1. **Your diet is healthy if...**
   A. *It contains no junk food or sweets*
   B. *If you're a vegetarian*
   C. *It contains a wide variety of food*

2. **I snack...**
   A. *When watching TV, at break times, on the way
      to school, when I am bored*
   B. *When I am hungry*
   C. *I don't snack between meals*

3. **How much water do you drink in a day?**
   A. *A glass with every meal*
   B. *I don't drink water but I do drink lots of
      fizzy drinks.*
   C. *8–12 glasses a day*

4. **The five-a-day phrase refers to:**
   A. *Five pieces of fruit
      and five pieces of
      vegetable a day*
   B. *Five portions
      of fruit and
      vegetables a day*
   C. *Five meals-a-day*

5. **What do you eat for breakfast?**
   A. Cereal with milk and sugar
   B. I don't eat breakfast
   C. Toast, eggs and a drink

6. **I eat fast food...**
   A. Once a day
   B. Once a week
   C. Once a month

7. **Chocolate should be eaten in moderation because ...**
   A. It's high in fat
   B. It causes bad spots
   C. You can get addicted to it

8. **What's the best way to reduce your risk of heart disease?**
   A. Reduce the amount of saturated fat in your diet because this is linked to heart disease
   B. Cut out all fat totally as it's bad
   C. Heart disease is hereditary so you can't do anything

9. **Which of the following contains sugar?**
   A. Bread
   B. Cereal bar
   C. Ready-made pasta
   D. Fizzy Cola
   E. Orange juice

10. *After you eat you often feel...*
   A. *Full of energy*
   B. *Sleepy and lethargic*
   C. *Bloated*

Scores

1.   A 5   B 10   C 0
A healthy diet is not a diet that divides foods into good and bad, but it is a diet that contains a wide variety of foods and also a little bit of what you like.

2.   A 10   B 0   C 5
A healthy diet should contain three meals a day and two snacks when you're hungry. Mindless snacking (snacking when you're bored or out of habit) is a big contributor to weight gain, so it pays to watch what you pick up and put in your mouth.

3.   A 5   B 10   C 0
The average person needs to drink around a litre and a half of water a day. Not only does it keep your organs hydrated but helps stop you feeling hungry and tired.

4.   A 5   B 0   C 10
Five-a-day is the recommended daily allowance of fruit and vegetables you should be eating. See below for more details.

5.   A 5   B 10   C 0
Never skip breakfast to lose weight. Studies show that people who avoid breakfast eat more at lunchtime and at breaks and so gain more weight.

6. A 10   B 5   C 0
Less is best when it comes to fast food, but you don't
have to give it up if you eat it in moderation.

7. A 0   B 10   C 5
Chocolate doesn't cause spots but it is high in fat so
should be eaten in moderation.

8. A 0   B 10   C 5
There are certain fats that are better for you than
others. To discover the difference, see the section about
saturated and unsaturated fats on page 84.

9.   Score 5 for every yes
All of these contain hidden sugars as sugar acts as a
preservative in food, just one reason why it pays to
read labels.

10. A 0   B 10   C 5
Good food equals energy, calorie
dense food causes lethargy.

Results
80–115
You may feel overweight, lethargic and unfit right
now, but you can change the way you look and feel
in a shorter time than you think. There are no
bad foods, just foods you should eat in moderation
e.g. high fat, high sugar foods like cakes, sweets and
crisps. Then there is the food you need to eat
for nutrients and energy e.g. fruit and vegetables,

carbohydrates and protein. Read on below for how to change your diet.

40–75
For optimum health, you need to ensure that you're making the right choices. With food, variation is the key. Healthy elements for a healthy diet should be based on lots of fresh and raw food, protein and carbohydrates and a little bit of what you like. Don't be too strict or you'll be tempted to revert to your old behaviour.

0–35
Congratulations! You're super-healthy and making good choices. However, remember not to be too extreme with yourself because this is the number one way to fall back into old habits. Always choose a wide variety of foods so you don't get bored with what you're eating.

A word about calories

You may have heard the word 'calorie' used and may not know what it is. It's basically the energy value of food and a way of measuring how much we should eat.

For instance the average calorie intake for a boy is:

Aged 11–14 years – 2,220 calories
Aged 15–18 years – 2,755 calories

For a girl it's:

Aged 11–14 years – 1,845 calories
Aged 15–18 years – 2,110 calories

To lose weight you need to create a calorie deficit by either reducing your calorie intake (eating less or eating healthier foods) or by increasing the amount of calories you burn (through exercise) or by doing both. It sounds a lot but it's not, because to lose a pound of body fat all you need to do is reduce your food intake or up your exercise intake by 3,500 calories a week. That's 500 calories a day.

To do this all you have to do is either forgo fast food (see step four below) and replace it with something healthy, or cut out a chocolate bar and a packet of crisps and walk for 30 minutes a day (at a relatively fast pace).

However, beware of becoming a mad calorie counter. Becoming obsessed with the calorie count of the foods you're eating is not the aim here. The aim is to be aware that what goes in needs to balance up with the amount of energy you burn.

A word about diets

"My sister swears by this diet that basically means you can lose 10lbs in one week by eating just cereal."

HANNAH, 14

You've probably heard it said a thousand times but it's true – faddy diets, miracle diets and diets based on getting rid of entire food groups don't work in the long run because they don't encourage you to eat healthily or in a way that you can eat for life. Once you stop dieting and start eating normally again you'll just regain all your weight.

While it's tempting to try a diet a friend swears by, remember that drastically cutting your calorie intake (something many diets do) makes your body cling onto every bit of food that you put into your body and then slow your metabolism down (see below), so you can't burn calories. Likewise, diets that promise huge weight loss every week are bad news. A healthy weight loss is 1–2lbs a week, any more and you risk feeling unwell and also regaining the weight lost very quickly. Just one more reason why healthy eating works and diets don't.

Metabolism

Your metabolism is the way your body burns calories – and the good news is you can crank it up to help your body be more efficient at weight loss. Here's how:

Eat regularly

Skipping meals is not good for the body's metabolism because after four hours without food, the body will suppress its ability to burn calories, in order to conserve energy. Drastically cut your calorie input further with a crash diet and your body will reduce its calorie burning potential by as much as 30%. What most people don't realise is that your metabolism rises when you eat because the body needs to burn energy for digesting and absorbing food.

Eat breakfast

Breakfast is the most important meal of the day especially as far as your metabolism is concerned.

This is because our metabolism naturally slows down when we sleep and won't work again until we eat. By-pass breakfast like a third of all British people and your body won't burn as many calories as it could do.

Think protein

Focus on protein to literally stoke your fat burning fires. Not only is it harder to digest (protein uses 20-30% more energy for digestion, an extra 150 to 200 calories a day) but it also forces your metabolic rate upwards. Mix it with good carbohydrates such as green leafy vegetables and fruit. This combination will dramatically change the way your body burns calories.

Go to bed earlier

A study from the University of Chicago shows that getting less than five hours sleep a night leads to the body over producing insulin, which in turn promotes fat storage. Sleep loss is also associated with alterations in hormone levels that regulate the appetite, so when you disrupt your sleep you end up wanting to eat more. Aim to get at least eight hours a night to keep the metabolism ticking over nicely.

Do some exercise

The good news is, no matter how slack you've been in the past it's what you do with your body now that will have a greater effect on your metabolic rate! This happens because lean muscle is an active tissue (unlike fat which does nothing but make you look big), so it basically eats up energy in your body. See chapter four for more ideas on exercising.

Vitamins and minerals

Vitamins and minerals are essential to our health but this doesn't mean going out and loading up on lots of supplements. A healthy diet will provide all the nutrients you need to help maintain general health and wellbeing but no single food contains the perfect mix of nutrients, which is why you need to eat a balanced and varied diet. Here's what you need:

Vitamin	Food Source	Good for
A	oily fish, eggs, dairy	healthy eyes
B	cereal, meat, bananas	helps release energy from food
C	oranges, strawberries	immune system
D	oily fish and cheese	healthy bones
E	avocado and nuts	healthy skin

Mineral	Food Source	Good for
Calcium	Milk, broccoli	bones and teeth
Iron	Fish, red meat, spinach	energy
Magnesium	Baked beans, pulses	energy
Zinc	Red meat, cheese	immune system

Why healthy eating isn't boring eating

"I hate vegetables, they make me feel sick."

LEANNE, 12

"I can't eat stuff like fruit, it's horrible."

JAMIE, 12

Say the words healthy food and it's likely that you'll think of all the things you don't like to eat. Things like vegetables, fruits, brown bread, milk and fish. Maybe you've never eaten these foods and have no idea how they taste, or you have tasted them once and hated them. Perhaps you have no idea how to cook them, or think it just takes too much effort to try them. But remember, all of the foods listed are staple foods – foods that act like a premium grade fuel to your body. Fill your body with these foods and you'll not only be bursting with energy but you'll lose weight too.

Do the opposite and pump your body with foods such as chips, burgers, pizza, biscuits and fizzy drinks and the opposite will happen to you – you'll feel tired, lethargic, depressed and you'll gain weight.

With weight loss the equation is simple – eat good foods, and you'll feel good. Eat fewer calories (the energy value of food) and expend more energy (through activity) and you'll lose weight. Eat food that screams variety and you'll fill your body with a variety of vitamins and nutrients that will not only make you look good, but you'll feel stronger and fitter.

Easier said than done, but when it comes to weight loss nothing quite works like a healthy diet because:

1. You'll never get bored by the choice of foods you can eat.
2. You'll be giving yourself a healthy food plan for life.
3. You can still have a little of what you like.

4. You'll be re-educating your taste buds so eventually you won't crave the foods that make you fat.
5. It's not expensive or difficult to find healthy foods so it's easy to make a healthy choice at breakfast, lunch and dinner.

Healthy eating is...
Eating a variety of foods
Having three meals a day and two snacks
Eating food for energy, as well as pleasure
Eating vegetables and fruit daily
Admitting that there are just some things you can't eat if you're trying to lose weight

Healthy eating isn't...
Eating fast food every day
Skipping breakfast to lose weight
Eating the same thing every day
Opting for a chocolate bar instead of a meal
Starving yourself

Weight loss myths

Contrary to popular belief the great majority of us are not made to be overweight, which means inside each and every one of us is a fit person eager to jump out. To allow this to happen you have to change your mindset by admitting you can do something about your weight.

Myth: Some people are just made to be fat.
Truth: Not true – none of us are genetically made to be fat, we become fat through bad lifestyle choices.

Myth: Never eat after 7pm as all the calories are then stored as fat.
Truth: It's not when you eat food but how much you eat overall that affects your fat levels.

Myth: Calories from fat make you gain weight faster than calories from carbohydrates.
Truth: Excess calories from any type of food make you gain weight.

Myth: I have a slow metabolism that's why I never lose weight.
Truth: Overweight people have a faster metabolic rate because their bodies need more energy to burn off food.

Myth: You can eat as much as you want if it's fat-free or low fat.
Truth: Fat free doesn't mean calorie free or sugar free, and low fat doesn't mean low calorie, so both can make you gain weight if you eat too much of them.

Myth: A vegetarian diet is less fattening.
Truth: Many vegetarians eat too much fat such as cheese (it gives their food flavour) making their diet just as unhealthy as that of a meat-eater.

Myth: Eating breakfast makes you hungrier.
Truth: Eating breakfast kick starts your metabolism, and helps you burn calories all morning.

Eight steps to losing weight

Step One: Listen to your hunger signals

Most of us practise mindless eating i.e. we eat and eat and don't notice what we eat or even stop to think if we're hungry or not. Sometimes it's because we're distracted by friends or the television, and other times it's pure habit or boredom. To lose weight and get fit you need to stop and think before you reach for food. Use the technique mentioned on page 25 and scale your hunger from one to 10 before you put something in your mouth.

Step Two: Eat more of these foods

To function properly, your body needs the right balance of foods and this means a good variety of foods, plenty of fresh food and less fatty ready-made products. Ideally make sure your diet is made up of 50% carbohydrates (vegetables, fruit and unrefined carbs like brown rice and wholemeal bread), 25% protein (lean meats, fish and eggs) and 25% unsaturated fats (nuts, seeds, oily fish). Here's what you should be eating every day:

CARBOHYDRATES – BROWN BREAD, RICE, CEREALS, POTATOES.

Carbohydrates are divided into refined (products that have had all the fibre taken out of them) and unrefined (products that still contain the fibre from the grain). For a healthy diet you need to eat more unrefined carbohydrates because these help your body process waste efficiently. Plus, unrefined carbohydrates keep you feeling fuller for longer and so you're less likely to reach for a snack an hour after eating.

Refined	Unrefined
White bread	Wholemeal and rye bread
Frosted cereal	Porridge (made from oats, not ready-made)
Cereal bar	Rice cakes
Tinned pasta	Wholemeal pasta

FRUIT AND VEGETABLES – FIVE PORTIONS-A-DAY

People who eat a lot of fruit and vegetables lower their risk of heart disease and cancer, which is why the World Health Organisation recommends that we all eat at least five portions-a-day. Apples, bananas and green leafy vegetables are particularly good as they are crammed full of vitamins and minerals and they also add fibre to your diet. If you hate the taste, stick with it because, unlike fast foods or ready-made foods, vegetables and fruits aren't crammed with extra sugars, salt and fat to pump up the taste. Give yourself time to get used to the flavours. A good way to do this is to try one new fruit or vegetable a day so you can find the ones you like best.

If you like sweet tasting foods try bananas, sweet potatoes, swede, oranges, red and green peppers, and melon.

If you like crunchy foods try broccoli, green beans, apples, pears, cucumber and radishes.

If you like soft pulpy foods try courgettes, mangoes, nectarines, peas and lentils.

A portion of fruit or vegetables is approximately 80g. This is the equivalent of a medium apple or banana, a bowl of mixed salad, a handful of grapes, or two to three tablespoons of vegetables (raw, cooked, frozen or canned). A portion of 100% fruit juice or fruit smoothy should be 150ml, but can only contribute one portion towards the five-a-day target, no matter how much you drink. The idea is to vary your diet with lots of different vegetables and fruits so you get fibre in your diet and as many vitamins and minerals as you can.

MILK AND CHEESE

Don't be tempted to ditch milk and cheese from your diet. Milk is essential for growing bodies as it's packed with vitamins and calcium, which are vital for growth, building strong bones and strong teeth. If you want to watch your weight go for semi-skimmed or skimmed milk as they contain exactly the same amount of calcium as the full fat variety. As for cheese - two matchbox sized portions are all you need a day as hard cheese is a form of saturated fat (see page 84), which in large quantities has been linked to an increased risk of heart disease. Under 18-year-olds need at least 800 to 1000mg of calcium a day.

Sources of Calcium	
0.2 litres of semi skimmed milk	230mg of calcium
0.2 litres of full fat milk	220mg of calcium
2oz of sardines	310mg of calcium
1oz of cheddar cheese	190mg of calcium
Small pot of yoghurt	285mg of calcium
115g of baked beans	60mg of calcium
115g of cottage cheese	80mg of calcium

PROTEIN – MEAT, EGGS, TOFU OR SOYA

These are essential because unlike fat, 1g of protein has less than four calories, whereas 1g of fat has nine calories. About 25% of your daily food intake should come from protein because it's essential for building bones, healthy teeth, hair and nails. The best sources are chicken, fish, soya products, milk and eggs. A diet rich in protein (as opposed to protein only) will also control your appetite and stimulate your hormones to burn fat in the body.

UNSATURATED FAT – OLIVE OIL, SALMON, TUNA AND SARDINES

Essential fatty acids, also known as unsaturated fat (fat that is liquid at room temperature – e.g. olive oil), is good for your heart's health. Oily fish, which are rich in Omega 3 and 6 essential fatty acids, should be added to your diet three times a week for maximum benefits.

Step Four: Eat less of the following

SATURATED FAT

A diet high in saturated fat (fat that's hard at room temperature like butter and cheese) can lead to heart disease and weight gain, and the bad news is that fat is often hidden in foods as it is the very thing that makes food taste good.

Reduce your intake of fried foods, biscuits, cakes, donuts, chocolate, cheese, fatty meats, pizzas and cream-rich pasta sauces.

FIZZY DRINKS

These drinks are laden with calories and sugars. In fact just one fizzy drink can have eight teaspoons of sugar, which makes them bad for your weight and your teeth. Even the 'diet' variety, are still high in acids, which are detrimental to your teeth and bones, plus most are full of caffeine, which gives you a quick high, followed by a low. Avoid them at all costs.

Swap a fizzy cola for a fruit smoothie. Fizzy drinks contain about 200 calories. Additive-free smoothies have the same calories but are full of vitamins and add towards your five-a-day count.

FAST FOODS

Burgers, pizza, chips, kebabs, chicken nuggets, fried chicken, fish and chips, sausage and chips, chips and chips, the list is endless and it all counts as fast food. This is the type of food that most people who need to get fit normally dine out on. If this is you, it's likely you do it because it's cheap and it tastes good. The bad news is that it's also calorie dense, full of sugar and guaranteed to make you fat if you eat it more than once a week.

Sadly if you're trying to get fit, it's this kind of food that you have to cut down on. If you're thinking of going to a fast-food place anyway but opting for a salad or a fish burger, well think again. Thanks to the bread, the dressings and the mayonnaise even the so-called healthy fast food isn't so healthy.

- Swap a ham and mushroom pizza and chips that contains 1,300 calories and 56g of fat for a vegetable pizza and salad containing 650 calories and 12g of fat.

- Swap two pieces of fried chicken, chips and coleslaw that come in at 985 calories and 58.3g of fat for a large chicken salad with oil dressing (not a cream-based one) which has 269 calories and 11.1g of fat.

Calorie Count of Fast Foods	
Big Mac with large fries	1150 calories
Burger King large fries	490 calories
Whopper Sandwich	670 calories
Kentucky Fried Chicken (breast)	410 calories
Pizza Hut, two slices of pepperoni pizza	520 calories

SNACKS (WITH HIDDEN SUGARS)

Crisps, chocolate bars, sweets, muffins, savoury snacks, cereal bars, flapjacks and brownies are just some of the foods you may be choosing to snack on. This is not good news for your body as they are all secretly pumping up your weight as most are rich in fat and sugar. While we all need snacks to get us through the day, this food doesn't add any value to your diet. Snack healthily by opting for one of the following:

- Swap a cereal bar or flapjack for oatcakes with peanut butter. Cereal bars or flapjacks are packed with hidden sugars, fats and additives, whereas oatcakes are low in calories and fat (only 1.3g per biscuit) and a small dollop of peanut butter adds protein.

- Swap chocolate and crisps for fruit and yoghurt. A 25g bar of chocolate contains 180 calories and 10g of fat, and a packet of crisps contains 160 calories and 10g of fat. Whereas, mixing berries with a pot of natural yoghurt adds to your five-a-day count and is vitamin packed.

SALT

It's not always easy to tell which foods contain large amounts of salt as high levels can be found in unlikely products such as bread, breakfast cereals and even pasta. In fact over 75% of our daily salt intake comes from salt hidden in processed food products such as

baked beans, spaghetti, ready-made meals and pizza, and not from the salt we add ourselves.

Having a high salt intake is bad for all of us because it's linked to high blood pressure, which is a contributing factor in over 170,000 deaths each year in the UK. To reduce levels of salt in your diet ensure that you start reading food labels to see the salt content of the food you're buying, cut down on salty snacks such as crisps and nuts, and avoid a diet high in processed foods.

Maximum recommended amount of salt per day	
AGE	**AMOUNT**
Up to 6 months	less than 1g a day
7–12 months	1g per day
1–3 years	2g per day
4–6 years	3g per day
7–10 years	5g per day
11–adults	6g per day

SUGAR

Like fat, sugar is a concentrated source of energy but it is calorie dense and because it usually goes hand in hand with fatty food, it's something to be avoided. Sadly most of the sugar we end up eating isn't what we add to our diet, but from hidden sugars in food. Look on food labels for signs of sugar also known as cane sugar, fructose, corn sweetener, dextrose, dextrin, corn syrup, maltose, sucrose, manitol or hydrolysed starch.

Step Five: Read food labels

One way to avoid hidden fats, sugars and extra calories is to know what's in your food, and the way to do this is to know your way round a label. For more information go to the Food Standards Agency website (see Resources on page 147).

LITE/LIGHT

These labels mean nothing and lead you to believe a food is healthy, but really it could simply mean the texture of the product is whipped to taste lighter. To find out if it's low calorie or low fat check it against the non-light version.

NO ADDED SUGAR

This doesn't mean what you're eating is sugar free, but that no sugar has been added to the sugar content that already exists within the product.

LOW FAT

The fat content is low, but be careful because this doesn't mean the product is low in calories as well.

LOW IN SUGAR

For a product to be low in sugar look for a label that says 2g per 100g.

REDUCED SALT

This does not mean the product you are eating is salt free but the product should have less than 0.25g salt (0.1g sodium) per 100g.

FRESH JUICE

Legally all drinks can use the word fresh and juice even if they contain as little as one per cent pure juice so check the label to see the actual percentage of real juice in your drink.

ADDED FIBRE

The product should have more than 6g per 100g.

REDUCED FAT

Reduced fat crisps have around 6.2g of fat per bag compared to the usual 12g per bag.

LOW CARB CHOCOLATE

Low carb chocolate bars contain less carbohydrate but have a high calorie and fat count so stay clear of them.

Step Six: Start with small changes

Small changes equal big differences. For instance, making your lunch box healthy can help cut your calorie intake by 500 a day. Studies show the average lunch box now contains around 1,100 calories – that's three-quarters of a your daily calorie intake – plus an entire day's salt allowance and 65g of sugar (13 teaspoons). Small changes lead to big results on the health front - here's how to do it.

- Swap a white bread sandwich for one made from wholemeal bread because it's got less sugar and more nutritious fibre and is only 60 calories a slice.
- Eat one less chocolate bar and drink one less glass of cola a day and you'll save 150 calories a day, that's 1,050 less calories a week.

- Watch how you or your mum cooks your food. Olive oil is good for you, but it's still oil, so don't load your pasta with it. Likewise, watch your salad dressings, mayonnaise and how you choose to cook your vegetables (boil or grill, don't fry).
- Eat your greens and your fruit. An apple has 75 calories and a 25g chocolate bar 180, which makes the fruit the better option for faster weight loss.

Step Seven: Watch your serving size

Eating wisely but still not losing weight? Well, you could be consuming bigger meals than you need. A serving is a handful, meaning a palm-sized piece of chicken or fish for your main meal.

A SERVING IS SMALLER THAN YOU THINK

One slice of large fruit like melon, pineapple or mango	= one serving
A small handful of dried fruit	= one serving
A side salad	= one serving
A medium sized apple	= one serving
Medium glass of fruit juice	= one serving
Half a cup of cooked vegetables	= one serving
Medium baked potato	= one serving
A medium bagel	= two to three servings
2-3 tbsp. of pasta	= one serving
Small pot of yoghurt	= one serving
Normal glass of milk	= one serving

Vegetables can be unlimited unless they are fried or coated in butter, in which case be careful. As for fruit, it is good for you, but not in large amounts as it's high in natural sugar. It is probably best to have two servings a day (one apple = one serving). Your five-portions-a-day rule should consist of two portions of fruit and three portions of vegetables.

If you're still confused try the hand guide to portion control:

- Meat/fish should be the size and thickness of your palm
- A piece of cheese should be the size and thickness of a matchbox
- Cereal or fruit should be the size of a clenched fist
- Pasta should be one cupped hand
- Salad should be two cupped hands

Step Eight: Drink more water

In these days of fancy coffee shops it's worth noting that an oversized cream topped, caramel coffee concoction can also add an extra 350 to 500 calories to your daily diet. If you're addicted to these drinks or to fizzy, sugary drinks, replace them by upping your water intake. Water will help keep you hydrated and drinking a glass of water before you eat also helps you to eat less at meal times.

Research shows one in five of us consume too little water throughout the day. The current recommendation is 1.5 litres of water (about eight to 10 glasses) per day. Not drinking this means most of us suffer from borderline dehydration every day, which equals tiredness and a tendency to snack for energy. Water is also vital for our optimum health. Not only does it hydrate organs and cushion the nervous system but it also stops you reaching for food when what you really want is a drink (thirst receptors often get mixed up with hunger receptors).

Ten ways to change your eating habits (without losing your mind)

1. Keep a food diary

If you feel you don't eat much and yet have gained weight (or haven't lost anything) then you need to take more notice of what goes into your mouth. That's every bite, every snack, every piece of food while you're cooking and every drink as it all counts. Keep a food diary for three days – you'll be surprised at how much you're really eating.

2. Eat slowly

Eat slowly to help your brain work out if it's eaten enough. Eat on the run and your stomach will still be 20 minutes behind your mouth, telling you you're hungry while food is already on the way.

3. Avoid diets

If your bookshelf is full of every diet book known to man, and you can recite who's been on the Eat No Carbohydrate, Drink Watercress Soup and Eat Like a Caveman diets then you're a diet junkie and need to go into diet rehab. Firstly toss away all those useless books, and make a promise to yourself that you won't ever be tempted by a ridiculous diet again. Think sensibly. For all the time and money you have ploughed into your diet book fixation you could have incorporated healthy eating tactics into your life, lost weight and saved yourself a ton of money.

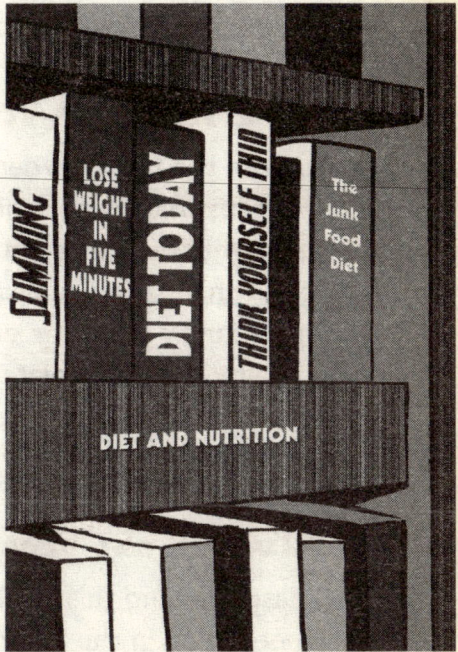

4. Don't compare yourself to others

This is the kiss-of-death to a good body image. If you're always looking at pictures of celebrities and negatively comparing yourself to them, it's worth remembering a few home truths. Firstly, most celebrities work and diet excessively to get the bodies you see in magazines. For most of them this means 5am runs, personal trainers, a rigid diet and no pudding. If you want their body you can get it, but do you really want to go through their regime?

5. Eat a little bit of what you like

Apart from the fact that denying yourself something you want just makes you think about it all the more, naughty delights such as chocolate aren't bad for you in themselves (unless of course you're going through a family sized bar everyday). For instance, good quality dark chocolate contains beneficial nutrients and won't make you gain weight unless you eat too much of it.

6. Always eat breakfast

The reason behind this thinking is simple - your body needs fuel in the morning because it hasn't eaten for at least 10 hours. Deprive it of food and it will run on empty and then retaliate at 11am and lunchtime and pretty much all day. Studies also show that skipping breakfast often leads people to eat more calories per day as they opt for a larger

lunch and more afternoon snacks. If you don't feel
hungry first thing, retrain your stomach by slowly
introducing food in the morning. Start with fruit
juice, then add a bowl of cereal.

7. Avoid boredom snacking

Walking around your kitchen casually opening
cupboards and the fridge and snacking on whatever
takes your fancy is the easiest way to consume 20
biscuits and 300 calories without realising it. Practise
your mum's best advice – always sit down and eat
off a plate so you can see what you're eating.

8. Carry snacks on you

The fastest way to eat a chocolate and a takeaway
pizza five times a week for dinner is to have no food
around when you're hungry. So make sure you carry
an apple in your bag during the day for when you
need a snack.

9. Don't super size

Chocolate bars and crisp bags are getting bigger
which is bad news for our thighs. The solution –
never buy larger sizes or family packs because you'll
only end up scoffing the lot. Funsize portions also
only work if you have huge amounts of willpower.
Stick to a normal bar, especially at the cinema where
we're all guilty of eating our way through a family
sized bag of sweets or a vat of popcorn.

10. Don't watch TV while you eat

Eating your meals while chatting on the phone, watching TV or reading a magazine is a sure way to not notice what you've eaten, and leave yourself feeling cheated and hungry for more. Limit your distractions, and you'll not only eat slower (allowing your stomach to register the fact it's no longer hungry) but also enjoy the process.

CHAPTER FIVE

Fit Bodies

Why get fit?

"I'm always the last to be picked for teams. I hate PE lessons."

TOM, 13

"I know I should do some exercise but I can't think what to do or where to do it."

LAURA, 14

Whether you're tall, small, fat, skinny or of a regular weight you need to be fit. This is because being fit is about lots of things such as being able to run for a bus without passing out, having confidence in your body image, looking good and generally feeling good about yourself. If that isn't reason enough to get fit, consider this — physical activity will not only make you feel fantastic but it will also help to control your weight for life, by using excess calories that would otherwise be stored as fat.

If you're worried about getting fit because you're not naturally sporty you're not alone. Doing any type of exercise is probably the last thing on your mind. If this rings true it's important to realise that getting fit isn't about being good at sport or being picked for teams but more about being active in your daily life, and that means doing more than taking regular strolls from the sofa to the fridge and back again.

Get fit and you'll...

- Reduce your risk of obesity using up any excess calories, which would otherwise be stored as fat.
- Build a healthy heart and reduce your risk of coronary heart disease. This is because exercise strengthens your heart muscle, helps lower your blood pressure and improves your blood flow, which increases your heart's working capacity.
- Build strong muscles and bones to help you feel better about yourself and your abilities and reduce the risk of chronic diseases in later life.
- Boost your body image because you'll increase your stamina, strength and flexibility.
- Reduce stress and anxiety and release feel good hormones to lift your mood.

These are just some of the reasons why everybody, no matter what their shape, size or age, should be exercising for the sake of their wellbeing. If you're under 18, government guidelines recommend that you do one hour of exercise every single day. It sounds daunting but the good thing is that exercise is cumulative, so you don't have to do it all in one go, but you can spread it in segments throughout the day. Either 20 minutes before school, 20 minutes at lunchtime and 20 minutes after school, or 10 minutes scattered six times through the day. For instance:

TIME	GET FIT ACTIVITY
10 mins	Walking to school instead of taking the bus
10 mins	Walking with friends at lunch time
20 mins	Walking home via the shops or the park
20 mins	Playing football, hockey or even dancing around your room

Commit to getting fit and...

1. IT WILL MAKE YOU LOOK LEANER

Fat takes up a lot more space in the body than lean muscle. One kilogram takes up five times as much space as 1kg of muscle. So if you exercise you'll change your shape dramatically.

2. IT WILL MAKE YOU FEEL HAPPY

A study from the University of New York Medical School found those who regularly worked out felt happier and more content than those who didn't. This is because the body releases endorphins - the body's natural painkillers – during activity, which will give you a natural high.

3. IT WILL STOP YOU GAINING WEIGHT

Muscle, unlike fat, burns calories. So, if you build up your muscle strength through exercise, your body will burn calories even when you're lying about.

4. YOU'LL START TO LOVE EXERCISE

The best news of all is that it takes just two weeks to make exercise a habit and six to nine weeks to then make it a part of your normal life. So, if you get active right now, it won't be long before your body and mind reap the benefits.

5. YOU'LL LOWER YOUR RISK OF HEART DISEASE

For the sake of your future health and well-being it's important to get fit as soon as possible. Apart from the fact it's easier to get fit when you're young, it's also easier to stay fit for life (overweight teenagers have a 70% chance of being overweight as adults), if you make activity a part of your every day life now.

Eating unhealthy foods and being unfit impacts on your future health by blocking your arteries and making your heart pump faster and harder. This causes high blood pressure and high cholesterol, which in turn are all linked to heart disease and type II diabetes. Currently well over 100,000 people die from heart disease in the UK each year.

People who are active are less likely to develop heart disease because exercise is good for the heart muscle and encourages good circulation to the heart. People who exercise regularly also tend to have a slower resting heart rate because their hearts are more efficient and healthy.

The non-fit excuses

"I start something but soon go off it. I can never seem to do it for long."

LISA, 14

"I have no time to do any exercise."

HARRY, 13

One of the biggest obstacles to getting fit is the uphill battle to get yourself off the sofa. So you should expect your first few attempts to be a struggle while your mind battles with a million reasons why you shouldn't do it. The good news is that each time you do it, it becomes easier and before long you will not only pass the 'I-don't-want-to-do-this barrier' but you will begin to love it (hard to believe right now but it's true). Here's how to bust the most popular 'can't-do' excuses.

'I haven't got time'

If you've got time to surf the Internet, play computer games and watch four hours of TV you have time to exercise. The key is time management. You need to either cut down on a sedentary pursuit (an activity where you're sitting on your bottom and not moving) or double up. For instance, see your friends but do something active with them like jogging around the park together or taking a trip to the local pool.

'I don't like it'

Most people don't like exercising at first, but that changes once you see the amazing things it can do to your body. Give it four weeks and we guarantee you'll start liking it.

'I'm worried that if I start and then stop all my muscle will turn to fat'

Muscle and fat are two different tissue types so if you stop exercising muscle doesn't turn to fat. If body fat increases it's for the same reason it does if you don't exercise at all i.e. because you're eating too much and you're not burning off excess calories.

'I don't have the energy'

Low energy has much to do with the food we eat and the lack of exercise we take (which is why it's hard to get up from the sofa if you've been lying there for two hours). Exercise more often and you'll feel less fatigued.

'I know thin people who don't exercise'

Exercise is not just about weight loss, which is why many slim people can also be unfit. Being fit means being able to run for a bus, walk up stairs and dance all night without feeling exhausted.

What's your fitness personality?

"I'm not the sporty team player type. I like doing things on my own"

JENNY, 13

"I wish I knew what I was good at because I am rubbish at football and I don't like doing exercise on my own"

TOM, 14

Of course, if you want to stick with the get fit programme, the obvious option is to go for something you'll enjoy and therefore will want to do. So, finding a form of exercise that matches your personality and fits in with your daily habits is the key to getting fit. Try the following quiz and find out how your personality and natural body type can help you to find the exercise that's best for you. Total your score after each section. The section in which you score the highest amount of Yes answers corresponds to your fitness personality.

(A)

Are you naturally wiry and lean?	**Yes/No**
Do you hate being told what to do?	**Yes/No**
Do you get bored and restless easily?	**Yes/No**
Are you naturally energetic?	**Yes/No**
Do you get stressed easily by other people?	**Yes/No**

Do you get annoyed if people hold you back? **Yes/No**
Do you hate watching sport on TV? **Yes/No**
Do team games frustrate you? **Yes/No**

Total Score:

(B)

Are you naturally of medium build? **Yes/No**
Are you competitive? **Yes/No**
Do you like to motivate others? **Yes/No**
*Do you get hyped up when watching
or playing sport?* **Yes/No**
Are you a bad loser in board games? **Yes/No**
Are you always raring to go? **Yes/No**
Do you like plotting to win? **Yes/No**
Do you prefer team games to solo pursuits? **Yes/No**

Total Score:

(C)

Are you naturally curvy? **Yes/No**
Do you find it hard to motivate yourself? **Yes/No**
Do competitive people annoy you? **Yes/No**
Are you happy whether you win or lose? **Yes/No**
Are you a naturally calm person? **Yes/No**
*Do you feel stressed when things get
too excitable?* **Yes/No**
Do you hate PE lessons? **Yes/No**
Are you a relaxed person? **Yes/No**

TOTAL SCORE:

TYPE A

If your fitness is off balance it's probably due to an unhealthy diet and no exercise. Your personality is actually geared to lots of activity and exercise because you're naturally energetic, and quick.

Fitness Options:
To get into the fitness groove, try power walking or running, both of which suits your energy packed nature. Also, give swimming a go to help build muscle, and skateboarding or a dance class for motivation. Avoid team games that are too competitive as you'll only get bored quickly.

TYPE B

You're naturally athletic looking but if that doesn't ring true then it's probably down to a sedentary lifestyle. An over reliance on coffee and snacks help keep you going, but these make you feel lethargic and overly tired.

Fitness Options
Key into your competitive and team mentality and give football, netball and hockey a go. If sports aren't your thing then choose to do something that you can excel in on your own or with a friend such as cycling, or power walking. Better still, get all your friends involved to help motivate yourself.

TYPE C

You're likely to be of average height, with a naturally curvy body. Your personality means you're an excellent team leader so use this to your advantage and start organising a fitness club with your friends.

Fitness Options
Any activity is good for your personality. Try swimming, home video work-outs and walking. Also try bike rides, long walks and even nights out dancing with friends to up your all round activity levels.

How to get active

"When I get home I am so tired all I do is lie on my bed until dinner."

EMMA, 13

If you want to be someone who feels excited and happy about life, you need to get active and be active. While exercise takes care of the get active bit, to be active you have to consciously make a decision to move about more often instead of relying on someone else to do it for you. So instead of moaning when your mum asks you to go back upstairs for something, or complaining because you're asked to come and hang out washing or do the washing up, do it and think of all the extra calories you're burning off in the process. The effect of always being ready to jump up at a moment's notice is that you'll find your body will be more geared up for activity. So you'll eventually be someone who initiates activity, rather than gets pulled into it.

To get active consider:

- Doing some housework like making the bed. Changing the sheets, turning the mattress and plumping up pillows burns around 50 to 80 calories.
- Helping out with the gardening (another big calorie burner) – this is also good for your back muscles.

- Leaving late for school and running to the bus stop each morning – this will burn around 100 extra calories a day.
- Standing up when you're on the phone talking to friends – this will increase muscle power and help you activate your stomach muscles.
- Offering to carry shopping home for your mum – better still, walk to the shops with her and increase both your muscle strength and cardiovascular fitness (see below).
- Volunteering to help with something around the house or at school.
- Running up and down the stairs. 10 minutes burns between 100 and 150 calories.

Get aerobic (and do your heart a favour)

"Exercise doesn't work for me. I never see results."
SARAH, 13

If the word aerobic conjures up images of Lycra clad women leaping around a gym class to music, think again. Aerobic exercise is simply any kind of exercise that takes effort and exertion and so requires lots of oxygen, breathing and heart pumping work. This is also known as cardiovascular fitness. It's this type of exercise that reduces the risk of heart disease, helps burn fat and makes us fit, which is why we all need to do an hour a day.

Cardiovascular fitness is all about improving the efficiency of your heart and lung muscles. In a fit person a run for the bus should be relatively easy and the recovery time (the time it takes for your breath and heart rate to return to normal) should be relatively short. In an unfit person the run will feel difficult, and breathing constricted.

Cardiovascular fitness is therefore an essential component of fitness and the only way to reach it is to get moving. Walk up stairs instead of taking the lift, jog, dance, run or even power walk. The aim is to exercise to a point where you will be breathing a little harder so your heart and lungs will be being exercised. The more cardiovascular exercise you do, the better your stamina and fitness will be.

If you think you already do enough aerobic exercise but can never see any results the chances are you're not hitting the right aerobic level for you. To work out if you're doing it correctly, you should always exercise to a level where you can speak, but wouldn't be able to sing. If you can't speak at all because you're gulping for breath, you are working too hard (and risk burn out i.e. you'll give up too soon). If you can sing quite happily or chat to a friend, you're not working hard enough and need to go faster in order to reap the benefits of doing exercise.

This is one reason why being on your feet all day isn't exercise and getting your PE kit on but then walking aimlessly around the gym doesn't work. Likewise, it's no good going for a walk if you walk so slowly that a snail could overtake you, or going swimming but spending 45 minutes chatting to your mates by the edge of the pool and 15 minutes floating on your back.

See the list of activities below for one that grabs your interest. If all of them sound dull or boring you need to give yourself a reality check about why you're sabotaging your chances of getting healthy. Possible reasons could be that you're too scared to try something new, you're afraid of making a fool of yourself and worried that you'll be laughed at, or you're anxious about being bullied for wanting to change your habits and get fit. All these things can hold us back from attempting to get fit, which is why you need to put these worries into perspective.

1. It's always scary trying out new things, if it wasn't nothing would ever be a challenge. The trick is not to wait until you're not scared (because this never happens) but to build up your courage and go for it anyway. Remember, if the fear stays with you, you can change what you're doing and stop. But, if you beat your reservations and fears by facing them, you'll have won and your confidence will soar.

2. Worrying about being humiliated is very common with exercise. Again the key is to think – so what? So what if you miss catching a ball, come last, fall over or even do something wrong in a game? Landing on your bottom is not the end of the world and it is often the only way we ever learn to do something. The good news is that feeling foolish is a momentary sensation, and once it's happened it's already in the past, which means forget it and move on.

3. As for being bullied about wanting to get fit, this is a problem you can do something about. Remember no true friend would ever ridicule you or make you feel bad about wanting to get fit and healthy so if they do it's likely that they are either afraid you're leaving them behind or they're too scared to do it themselves. If you're being bullied tell a parent, older sibling or teacher what's going on and ask them to intervene before it gets out of hand.

Aerobic exercise is...

Dancing
Swimming
Team games like football
or hockey
Power walking
Running/Jogging
Rollerblading

Skipping
Doing a work-out video at home

Get strong – strength training exercise

"I am really skinny and thin and I'd love to get more muscle and look stronger."

GAVIN, 13

Toning and strengthening your muscles is an essential part of exercising and getting fit because not only does more lean muscle in your body mean less body fat, it also means you will be stronger for longer. This is because muscle is an active tissue (unlike fat which does nothing but make you look big), so it basically eats up energy in your body. The more overall muscle you have, the more strength you will have and the more energy you will burn (meaning you can eat more food and not gain weight, or eat more healthily and lose weight).

Contrary to popular belief this type of training is not just for boys, and if you're a girl doing it, it won't make you look bulky or give you big muscles (men get beefy because they have higher levels of the hormone testosterone which helps build muscle). It will however, make you feel stronger, look leaner and generally keep your body in a good working condition for life.

Strength and resistance training exercises are:

Martial arts
Yoga and Pilates
Tennis
Badminton
Press-ups on your bedroom floor
Swimming

A strong muscular body means:

- Stronger bones (and less risk of osteoporosis when you're older)
- More energy – the stronger you are, the more your body can cope with on a daily basis
- A better mood – thanks to an endorphin release from working out
- A loss of inches – as muscle takes up less room than fat in the body
- Better stamina

Ten get fit fast options

Running

Running works on boosting fitness because it's cardiovascular exercise. Such exercise is essential for fitness as it lowers your risk of a serious disease, burns body fat and generally keeps you fit. Running is also a huge calorie burner as you can burn nearly 500 calories in just 45 minutes. It also makes you leaner, sculpts your leg muscles, firms your bottom and is an amazing stress reliever. However, if you're like many people out there, you're probably thinking of skipping the running bit because you're positive you can't run or that you are not a natural runner.

Marathons across the world show everyone can run, no matter what their PE prowess at school or their size. All it takes is preparation, effort and patience. Here's how to get your running legs on:

1. Wear decent running shoes that support your feet.
2. Run with a friend for support.
3. Don't overdo it at first. Walk for two minutes, run for two minutes and repeat for 30 minutes.
4. Don't run too fast. This is the mistake most people make. It's not a race, or a sprint, but a run, so the aim is to run at a moderate pace, so you can run for longer.
5. Run heel to toe. Hit the ground with your heel, roll your foot forwards and spring off your toes.
6. Take water with you and drink it regularly.
7. Stop if you feel a sharp pain anywhere.
8. Stretch for five minutes before you run and five minutes after your run.

Walking

Walking is a fantastic form of exercise. It's cheap, easy to do and according to the British Heart Foundation all it takes to get fit is just 10,000 steps a day. If you think that sounds too much, just take a walk around your house, or down the road to a friend's house and see how many steps you clock up (it's more than you think).

Walking your way to health works because walking not only improves cardiovascular fitness but also increases your strength and tones your muscles.

To walk effectively, make sure you're wearing good trainers, and that you walk at a moderate pace, so you're not so out of breath you can't even say your name.

Swimming

Swimming properly (that's swimming without stopping for a chat, and using the right technique) improves upper and lower body strength as well as aerobic strength. It's also cheap and can be easily done at your local pool. With swimming the big problem most people have is getting their breathing right, especially when doing front crawl. This means they either hold their breath for too long and exhaust themselves, try to breathe in and out while their head is out of the water, or swim with their

head out of the water, thereby putting a strain on
their neck. To get your breathing right, the key is to
slowly breathe out under the water, and when you
turn your head breathe in. Other good swimming
tips are:

1. Keep your strokes long and steady.
2. Don't kick too hard.
3. Use the whole of your leg to kick, not just your
    feet and calves. This will push you further ahead
    and also work your stomach.
4. Practice your breathing and long leg kicks with
    a paddleboard until you get it right. Or try
    another stroke that works for you, such as
    breast-stroke.

Cycling

Cycling is a great form of exercise because it
works all your leg, bottom and stomach muscles.
As tempting as it is, don't rely on momentum to
get you around. This is where you sail down hills,
and let the gradient do all the work for you. The
aim with cycling is to put some effort in, so go at a
steady pace and challenge yourself with some hills
to get the cardiovascular benefits.

1. Make sure your saddle is at the right height.
    When you're pushing down, your leg should be
    extended with your knee slightly bent.

2. When you cycle, your upper body shouldn't wobble around or move from side to side, all the work should come from your legs. To stop the wobble, pull in your stomach to support you (imagine pulling your belly button to your spine).

3. Keep your neck and shoulders relaxed by not gripping the handlebars too hard.

4. Wear protective clothing, especially if you're mountain biking.

Aqua aerobics

Contrary to its image, aqua aerobics is not just for old ladies. Its benefits include fat burning, a boost to the metabolism, major resistance work and an increase in your heart and lung capacity. Other good news is aqua classes are different for everyone as they can be adapted to all levels of fitness. If you have an injury, or are a beginner the exercises can be slower and more specific. A typical class lasts around 45 minutes and is usually divided into three key stages – the warm up, the aerobic element and then toning.

1. For classes near you check out your local leisure centre
2. Bring water to drink, as aqua aerobics is thirsty work
3. Don't overdo it at the beginning
4. Don't cheat just because the instructor can't see you properly

Power walking

Power walking is walking at a brisker pace than normal and in a more energetic way than you would if you were simply taking a stroll to the shops. To do it right, put on your trainers and aim to go for a long walk. Start off at a gentle pace and build up to a vigorous walk. Pump your arms up and down as you go to help drive you forwards and to work

your arm muscles. Do it right and it will tone
your thighs, calves, bottom and stomach and also
burn calories and fat. It's good for increasing your
stamina and cardiovascular power.

1. Power walk with a friend for extra motivation
2. Wear trainers not shoes
3. Take water along, as it's thirsty work
4. Don't power walk alone with headphones on

Dancing

Dancing is a great way to get fit. If organised classes
aren't your thing, simply turn up the radio and
dance around your room. Always aim to dance
continuously for at least 10 minutes and sorry,
slow dancing doesn't count. Apart from the obvious
aerobic benefits to your heart and lungs, dancing
also helps increase muscle strength, promote
flexibility (how bendy your body is) and improve
posture and balance. Better still, the movements
can also help tone and strengthen parts of the legs,
stomach, and back.

1. Good dancing classes are belly dancing, jazz
   dance, ballet, tap dancing and salsa. Check out
   your local leisure centre for classes
2. The higher the tempo (pace and speed) of the
   music, the more motivated you'll feel to dance
3. Time yourself so you know you're clocking up
   the right amount of minutes

Park games

You may not be a fan of playing football in the park but consider other aerobic style games you and your friends could try. Frisbee throwing, rounders, and even tag games count. Aim for 20 minutes of continuous exercise to get the full benefit, and make sure you jog on the spot if you're waiting for your turn. Aside from the enjoyment factor, all park games increase cardiovascular strength, build muscle strength and burn fat. Expect an added bonus of an increase in co-ordination, balance, strength and stamina.

1. Get some props – a frisbee, football, tennis ball and a bat are essential park game items
2. During the week, set-up games at lunch-time in your school grounds
3. Don't be too competitive – the aim is to get fit not to always win

Skateboarding

Ask any skater and you'll soon discover skate-boarding is about more than doing fancy flips and turns in the air. Finding your stance on a board requires muscle strength, balance and stability. Once you get the hang of it, it's excellent for cardiovascular strength and self confidence. Riding a board also builds strong legs, firm thighs and good overall strength.

1. Visit a local skate park to see if it's for you
2. Ask advice in any skate shop for the best beginners board and tips on how to start
3. Always wear protective gear to help avoid injury

Alternative sports

Take a class in a martial art, try boxing or ice-skating, or consider something really different like Brazilian street fighting. The list of alternative activities you can do to get fit is endless and not always wildly expensive. Look for your nearest class on the Internet and, depending on your sport of choice, you'll be toning muscles, increasing your heart and lung power and increasing your self esteem by trying something new and daring.

1. Alternative sports can be tailored more towards your strengths
2. They boost your self esteem
3. They increase the excitement and adrenalin factor because they rely on your inner strengths

A note about safety

Before doing sports of any kind it's essential to seek medical advice. If you are on medication, have an existing injury or you are very overweight your GP will need to give you the official go ahead. This is because exercise puts a large exertion on your heart, which is already pumping extra hard if you are overweight so you need to take care. When ready be sure to:

1. Wear proper trainers – they don't have to be the latest and coolest but they should give you proper support.
2. Warm up before doing something strenuous – five minutes brisk walking should warm up your muscles sufficiently.
3. Drink water as you exercise – this stops dehydration and will keep you going. Sports drinks are full of sugar and should be avoided unless you're about to run a marathon.
4. Stretch after exercising and hold each stretch for 30 seconds – if you skip this you leave yourself at risk of injury and aches and pains.
5. Stop if you feel a sharp pain (a dull, stretchy ache is just your muscles working).
6. Never exercise if you are unwell, it won't speed your recovery.

Ten ways to get the most out of exercise

Take before and after pictures

This is a great way to measure your success and to notice how quickly your body is changing. Take the pictures monthly for best effect and in the same article of clothing so you can see how your body is changing. Also keep an exercise journal and note down what's changed and what you've noticed about your body in terms of toning up, loss of inches and increased strength. Remember, this is your personal motivation tool, you don't have to show it to anyone else.

Don't skip the hard bits

When exercising it's always tempting to stick to the parts you love and know you're good at and ignore the rest. In most cases this means giving the hard aerobic element a miss and focusing on stretching or fancy football moves. As easy as this is to do, remember that to lose weight and get fit you need regular breathless exertion to keep your heart working and your body burning calories. Break the aerobic part up so that you can reward yourself with your favourite bits to keep you going.

Set attainable goals

Set exercise goals that will spur you on and won't have you reaching for a packet of chocolate biscuits three days after starting out of boredom or despair. Good weekly goals include making yourself

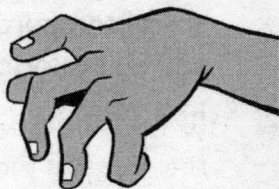

exercise for an hour a day, walking to school or even going outside at lunch times. Good monthly goals include a weight loss figure, a noticeable change in your fitness levels or clothing size.

Eat before you exercise

It's important to always eat before doing any exercise because it's a myth that you'll burn more calories if you're hungry when you start. Exercise on an empty stomach and you'll feel faint because your body will have no energy to burn. Eat a light snack (not a heavy fatty meal) an hour before you work out for optimum results. Choose a fruit smoothie, a banana or a piece of toast with peanut butter.

Drink more water to work out harder

The body also craves more water when it's working hard. Aim to drink two glasses of water around an hour before you exercise, and sip small amounts as you exercise to top levels up and avoid dehydration. Dehydration can appear as a headache, a feeling of being dizzy and faint. Avoid sugar-based, so-called 'sports' drinks, these just sap your energy and add calories you don't need. Water works just as a well.

Adapt your routine

The body adapts quickly to an exercise routine, especially aerobic work, so be sure to either change your aerobic activity regularly or keep challenging yourself to try something new to keep boredom at bay. Try a variety of sports such as running, football, skipping, swimming, cycling or a dance class.

Focus on what you're doing

Exercise studies show you can maximise the benefits by concentrating your mind on the muscles you're working. This means that you need to stop thinking about the time or what's on TV as you exercise, and focus instead on each muscle and your breathing for maximum benefits.

Listen to music

Listening to music you love while you work out can help to push you to work harder. Stick to fast-paced dance CDs instead of slow pop tunes to rev you up and get you going.

Don't forget to breathe

It sounds silly but most of us forget to breathe when we're concentrating on something difficult. If you feel dizzy or light-headed after one move, the chances are you need to breathe more. Inhale to lift a weight and exhale to lower.

Don't take too many rest breaks

If you're aiming to exercise for 10 minutes straight, don't stop to rest until 10 minutes are up, otherwise you lose the effect. Longer work out times and shorter recovery periods (where you try to get your breath back) are better for your heart's health.

CHAPTER SIX

The Fit Plan

Hopefully by this stage of the book you're armed with all the facts you need to get fit. The aim of this chapter is to give you an idea of how to go about incorporating exercise and healthy eating into your daily life. It's not a diet plan, but an idea plan. Follow it word for word if you want to or mix the ideas into your own life. Remember, to get fit you need to be honest about what you're eating and how much you're exercising. However, if you slip up every now and then it's not the end of the world. Don't give up, just make tomorrow a better day.

Before you start THE FIT PLAN make sure you have done the following:

1. Spoken to your mum (or whoever does the cooking and shopping) about your aims, why you're doing it and what she can do to help you to stick to it (chapters two and four).
2. Bought an exercise journal ready to note down your goals (chapter two) and what you do each day (chapter five).
3. Have a bottle of water on hand so you can keep drinking when exercising to stop your body becoming dehydrated.

4. Have some workout clothes and trainers. They don't have to be the latest fashion, but you do need a pair of trainers that support your feet and so help you avoid injury.
5. Have chucked out all the tempting foods that might sabotage your healthy eating plan (chapter four).
6. Have a clear plan of what you're going to do and why (chapters two and five).
7. Know your start weight (or clothing size).
8. Know your start fitness rating (i.e. how far you can walk without feeling out of breath).
9. Have people who can help support and advise you – your parents, PE teacher, your friends, and your GP.
10. Are being realistic about your goals (chapter one and two).

Exercise – the key points

As we said earlier, any exercise is better than none. Doing such things as walking or cycling to school or to friends' houses instead of going by car or bus will help you get fit. Try walking up stairs as a habit instead of using the lift or getting off the bus a stop early to walk the rest of the way to school. This all helps because a general attitude of more activity and less lying around helps get you into a fit mindset.

Before you start, always warm up first with gentle bends and stretches and then gradually build up to more vigorous exercise. As your fitness improves also remember to challenge yourself during your exercise so that you end up with the best results.

The best time to exercise

The best time to get moving is usually the time when you know you'll actually do it. For most people this means first thing in the morning so they can get it over and done with. However, if you're not an early bird forget this. Instead, think of something you do everyday without fail – such as lie on the sofa watching TV. This is the ideal time to spend one hour exercising. If you want to divide your exercise into segments in terms of your body's cycle, the following times of day are best for certain results:

7–9am
Early morning workouts will kick-start your metabolism, and keep you burning calories all day.

12–2pm
Exercise before lunch, not afterwards, otherwise you'll feel too sluggish to move.

3-5pm
This is a good time to do competitive sports as research shows this is when your co-ordination is at its highest.

7-9pm
The body is warmed up and flexible so you'll have greater stamina, and strength, so it's a good time to build muscle.

9–12pm
Your body's winding down – don't exercise!

Use a work card
It's important to chart your achievements so you know how far you've come. Use this weekly exercise workcard to log all the exercise you've done so you can see how you're doing.

WEEKLY EXERCISE WORKCARD

Activities DAYS	1	2	3	4	5	6	7
Power Walking/Walking MINUTES							
Dancing MINUTES							
Park Games MINUTES							
Swimming MINUTES							
PE Class MINUTES							
Cycling MINUTES							
Other Sports MINUTES							
Running MINUTES							**TOTAL**

Food – the key points

You should know exactly what healthy eating means
by now, but here's a quick recap of what you need
to do to lose weight.

- Eat five portions-a-day of fruit and vegetables
  and salad (but not potatoes)
- Drink 1.5 litres of water a day
- Cut out or limit the following:
    Processed ready-made meals
    Chocolate
    Cakes and biscuits
    Crisps
    Fast food
    Fizzy drinks
    White bread
    Processed cheese
    Fruit flavoured drinks
- Don't starve yourself – you should never be
  hungry
- Watch your portion size
- Count everything you eat, no matter how small
  (better still, keep a food diary)
- Allow yourself the occasional treat (see the
  sample food plan in this chapter)
- Don't let anyone act like the food police –
  make your own decisions and be responsible
  for yourself
- Always choose lean cuts of meat about the size
  of your palm

- Be aware of how food is cooked. Try not to eat food that is fried, has added butter or is drowned in oil and dressings
- Don't multi-task and eat. If you eat too fast, or when you're stressed or while watching TV you won't chew food properly
- Eat breakfast every day

Sample menus

To help you eat the right amount of food use the hand guide to portion control (see page 91).

7 BREAKFAST OPTIONS (CHOOSE ONE-A-DAY)

- Two scrambled eggs, one slice of brown toast and two rashers of grilled bacon
- One grilled sausage with two boiled eggs and a piece of wholemeal toast
- A bowl of porridge with one piece of fruit
- A two egg omelette filled with a small spoon of low fat soft cheese and ham (two slices)
- Two poached eggs, a handful of grilled mushrooms and two grilled tomatoes
- Two slices of wholemeal toast with a teaspoon of peanut butter (no extra butter)
- A bowl of cereal (with no sugar frosting or added chocolate bits), milk, a slice of wholemeal toast with marmite or jam

7 LUNCHES (CHOOSE ONE-A-DAY)

- Chicken (a piece no bigger than the palm of your hand), a small jacket potato with as many vegetables as you can eat and a mixed green salad
- Tuna or salmon, preferably grilled not fried (a piece no bigger than the palm of your hand), with salad and a serving of pasta
- Roasted vegetables, two portions of cheese (matchbox sized) and half a cup of rice
- Small can of tuna fish, prawns or seafood mix and a mixed salad in a medium baked potato
- Chicken tikka pieces (it should fill the palm of one hand) with a cucumber and tomato salad and a tablespoon of rice
- Tomato based sauce and a serving of pasta, with a sprinkling of cheese (one matchbox size)
- A brown bread sandwich with turkey, chicken or beef, and a salad made up of lettuce, avocado, tomatoes and cucumber

7 DINNERS (CHOOSE ONE-A-DAY)

- Chicken kebabs with stir-fried broccoli and mushrooms, and a jacket potato
- Grilled steak, spinach and mushrooms, a cup full of boiled potatoes and a side salad
- Oven roasted vegetable pizza (use at least 7 different vegetables), and a small amount of mozzarella and tomato salad

- Grilled chicken breast (a piece no bigger than the palm of your hand), with grilled vegetables and mashed potato, cauliflower and carrots
- Grilled salmon (a piece no bigger than the palm of your hand), spinach, carrots and mashed potato with low fat yoghurt (not butter)
- A 4oz burger, oven chips (a handful) and a large salad
- Tandoori chicken (a piece no bigger than the palm of your hand), two tablespoons of plain rice and a salad

7 HEALTHY SNACK CHOICES (ONE OR TWO A DAY)

- Two slices of wholemeal bread with a small pot of cottage cheese or a teaspoon of peanut butter
- One medium apple (it should be the size of a tennis ball)
- Three plums
- Two crispbreads with low fat cheese or a teaspoon of peanut butter
- 1 crumpet topped with low fat cheese and a small chopped apple
- 25g of popcorn (no butter)
- 1 small banana

The get fit food and exercise plan

Monday

Breakfast
Choose from the breakfast options on page 132.

10 minute activity
Power walk for 10 minutes to school.

Mid morning snack
Swap a large bag of crisps for a medium banana for energy.

Lunch
Choose from the lunch options or make sure your lunch contains a salad or vegetables, a piece of fruit, and some form of protein (meat, fish, cheese).

20 minute activity
Football or a brisk walk.

Afternoon snack
Swap a chocolate biscuit (74 cals) for a jaffa cake (36 cals).

10 minute activity
Walk round to a friend's house, or walk home.

Dinner
Choose from the dinner options.

20 minute activity
Dance around your bedroom, go outside for a game with friends, or go for a cycle ride.

Tuesday

Breakfast
Choose from the breakfast options.

10 minute activity
Cycling to school or around the block before school.

Mid morning snack
Swap a large bag of crisps (250 cals) for a medium banana (133 cals).

Lunch
Choose from the lunch options.

20 minute activity
A game of football or a walk around the shops or playing fields.

Afternoon snack
Swap a pastry (280 cals) for a bagel (185 cals).

30 minute activity
A work out video at home, or swimming with friends.

Dinner
Choose from the dinner options.

Wednesday

Breakfast
Choose from the breakfast options.

Mid morning snack
A medium sized apple.

Lunch
Choose from the lunch options.

30 minute activity
Park games, a long lunchtime walk or join a lunchtime sports club.

Afternoon snack
Swap a chocolate bar (180cals) for 3 Jaffa cakes (108 cals).

30 minute activity
Swimming with friends, an exercise class or a home work out video.

Dinner
Choose from the dinner options.

Thursday

Breakfast
Choose from the breakfast options.

10 minute activity
Power walk to school.

Mid morning snack
A small packet of nuts.

Lunch
Choose from the lunch options.

20 minute activity
Power walk with friends.

Afternoon snack
Swap a bag of crisps (200 calories) for a fruit smoothie (150 cals).

30 minute activity
Power walk home.

Dinner
Choose from the dinner options.

Friday

Breakfast
Choose from the dinner options.

10 minute activity
Run up and down the stairs at home.

Mid morning snack
Swap a sausage roll (370 cals) for two crumpets (140 cals).

Lunch
Choose from the lunch options.

10 minute activity
Power walk with friends.

Afternoon snack
A piece of fruit.

30 minute activity
Football or swimming

Dinner
Choose from the dinner options.

Saturday

Breakfast
Choose from the breakfast options.

10 minute activity
Walk to a friend's house or to the shops.

Mid morning snack
Swap a croissant (266 cals) for a low fat yoghurt
(90 cals).

Lunch
Choose from the lunch options.

40 minute activity
Play a game of football, or walk around the shops
with friends, cycle ride, park games.

Afternoon snack
Swap ice cream (200 cals) for 100% fruit lolly
(70 cals).

Dinner
Choose from the dinner options.

Sunday

Breakfast
Choose from the breakfast options.

20 minute activity
Do something totally different from the rest of the
week like dance round your room; help with the
housework or in the garden.

Mid morning snack
A small bar of chocolate.

Lunch
Have a Sunday lunch but go slow on the potatoes
and portion sizes.

40 minute activity
Go for a long walk with your family.

Afternoon snack
A slice of fruit loaf.

Dinner snack
Depending on how much you had at lunch vary
what you're eating now.

And finally ...

Whether you're still mulling the plan over or have thrown yourself in to it, be sure to make it fun. If you choose activities that are enjoyable and challenging, you'll see faster results and you'll be motivated to keep it up.

As for those bad days where you slip up and can't bring yourself to exercise or you crave something unhealthy, give yourself a break. What matters is what you do in the long run. It's about how you choose to live your life on the whole, not what happens when you opt out for a day. A fit lifestyle should be a happy lifestyle that leaves you feeling healthy and good about yourself. It should not be guilt ridden and miserable, otherwise your good intentions won't last.

As for getting fit, remember, you can do it! No matter what other people say, what the scales currently read or how many times you've tried and given up in the past, you have the ability to get in shape. Give it a try, what have you got to lose?

Resources

General health and fitness

BBC Health – www.bbc.co.uk/health
For tips and advice on exercise and healthy eating

Healthy Living – www.healthyliving.gov.uk
An NHS Scottish site on exercise and healthy food

British Heart Foundation www.bhf.org.uk

Healthy eating

British Nutrition Foundation www.nutrition.org.uk

British Dietetic Association www.bda.uk.com

Department of Health www.dh.gov.uk

Food Standards Agency www.food.gov.uk

Fitness

Dance Classes in the UK - www.learntodance.co.uk

Sport England
3rd Floor Victoria House
Bloomsbury Square
London WC1B 4SE
Tel: 08458 508 508
www.sportengland.org

Sport Scotland
Caledonia House
South Gyle
Edinburgh EH12 9DQ
Tel: 0131 317 7200
www.sportscotland.org.uk

Sports Council for Wales
Sophia Gardens
Cardiff CF11 9SW
Tel: 029 2030 0500
www.sports-council-wales.co.uk

Sports Council for Northern Ireland
House of Sport
Upper Malone Road
Belfast BT9 5LA
Tel: 028 9038 1222
www.sportni.org

English Federation of Disability Sport
Manchester Metropolitan University
Alsager Campus
Hassall Road
Alsager ST7 2HL
Tel: 0161 247 5294
www.efds.co.uk

Scotland Federation of Disability Sport
www.scottishdisabilitysport.com
 Northern Ireland Federation of Disability Sport
www.dsni.co.uk
Wales Federation of Disability Sport
www.disability-sport-cymru.co.uk

Advice and help

The Site www.thesite.org

Childline 0800 1111

National Centre for Eating Disorders
Tel: 01372 469493
www.eating-disorders.org.uk

The website addresses (URLs) included in this book were valid at the time of going to press. However, because of the nature of the Internet, it is possible that some addresses may have changed, or sites may have changed or closed down since publication. While the author and publishers regret any inconvenience this may cause the readers, no responsibility for any such changes can be accepted by either the author or the publisher.

Index